the plant room

the plant room

Joe Swift

Dedicated to Cathy, Stanley & Constance

Published by BBC Worldwide Limited,
Woodlands, 80 Wood Lane,
London W12 0TT

First published in 2001
Copyright © Joe Swift 2001

ISBN 0 563 55189 5

Commissioning Editor Vivien Bowler

Cover Art Directon Pene Parker

Book Art Directon Lisa Pettibone

Designer Mark Latter, Vivid

Project Editor Vicki Vrint

Copy Editor Emma Callery

Set in Officina
Printed and bound in Great Britain by Butler & Tanner Ltd, Frome and London
Colour separations by Radstock Reproductions Ltd, Midsomer Norton

For information about this and other BBC books, please visit our website on www.bbcshop.com/bbc_shop

Previous page: **In a city garden there is a close connection between the interior and exterior of a property. The materials used here seamlessly link the spaces together to create a real indoor/ outdoor space.**

contents

introduction

In the cosmopolitan setting of a modern international city such as New York, London or Sydney there is an exciting shift taking place within the gardening world. This shift is a reflection of modern urban living and the new demands put on to a city garden. A combination of issues has led to a more multifunctional approach with the outdoor space becoming much more flexible in its use. As well as a garden having to look good all year round, it has also increasingly become seen as an extra room to the house: somewhere to relax, entertain, cook, eat, play and work.

There is a particular energy found only within the city, which becomes reflected in its garden life. The diverse range of cultural influences and lifestyles makes a fertile environment for innovation and creativity. The cultural melting pot of the urban environment encourages an eclectic approach to garden design. Strictly thematic gardens such as a pure Japanese garden or a Mediterranean garden can look good in their native surroundings but often sit awkwardly and feel out of place in the vibrant

Previous pages: **The garden is an extra room to the house. Modern garden design allows people to create a functional but exciting outdoor space.**

Below: **Modern materials such as metal and glass look good in a contemporary garden. This feature works well as a sculpture by day and doubles as an intriguing light fitting to keep the interest at night.**

setting of a modern city. Through this crossover between functionality and creativity, combined with a fusion between the gardens of different cultures, there is a whole new garden style emerging. This style is highly creative and is breaking the mould of the more formal and traditional approach to garden design. This book helps to define this new style as well as – I hope – inspiring readers to be creative and experimental with their own outdoor space.

Being fortunate enough to have an outdoor 'room' – however small – in the city is a real luxury. In the past the garden was viewed as a place to primarily grow plants, but to use this premium space as somewhere just to

grow plants seems such a waste. Certainly the plants are important, but they are only one of many elements that go in to creating a successful garden. No longer is the garden being viewed as simply a place to imitate or re-create nature. The city itself is so far detached from the natural landscape that to me this approach seems logical. Gardens and plants can be a way for urban dwellers to reconnect with nature, but an overly naturalistic garden feels out of place within a city setting. The visual terms of reference within a metropolis are likely to be a combination of structural materials such as steel, concrete, glass or brick mixed with some softer planting elements. It follows that a blend of fabricated elements and plants, when used in a deliberate and planned way, will integrate the garden into the city in a more invigorating and harmonious fashion.

Above: Awkward small spaces can be the only garden a city dweller may have. Here the sculptural cordylines, chamaerops and agaves are combined to create an all-year-round composition.

A place in which to spend leisure time

Time is one of the major factors when planning a garden today. The stresses within the city mean people have always been pushed for the luxury of time, but it is possible to have a great garden without spending hours and hours weeding and mowing the lawn. It is impossible to fully unwind in a garden where there's lots of work to be done. There are many new products on the market such as computerised irrigation systems, weed-suppressing mats and mulches which, combined with general good planning, will all help to reduce the amount of maintenance required. A garden owner can now actually dictate the amount of time they'd like to spend and on which part of their garden they'd like to spend it.

Recently, the gardening world has become linked to other types of 'lifestyle' categories. There is no doubt that architecture and interior design are clearly connected, but food, cookery and fashion are now all more closely linked to the garden. The garden has become a place of fusion. As lifestyles become more diverse and choices are greater so the outdoor space has become a place to reflect one's personality and individual taste.

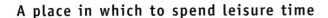

In the past, gardening has been seen as a more elderly pursuit, but recently it has become much more popular among the younger generations. It is because gardening can be taken on so many different levels that it is so appealing to so many people. I think it is fabulous the way gardening cuts across so many different levels within society. Barriers, which are created from differing levels of income, race, class and age, can be helped to break down by gardening. Of course, there are financial restrictions for everyone, but imagination and creativity are the most important things when making a garden.

The garden has become a priority for many when looking to rent or buy properties in the city. Whether it's a tiny backyard or a large city garden the feeling of freedom even a small outside space can bring to one's life has become an absolute essential to many city dwellers. In the heat of the summer the garden can be the perfect antidote to the stresses of urban living. Knowing that there is a cool, calm retreat to escape to at the end of the day can help to get you through the most hectic of days.

The outdoor room

There is no doubt the movement towards the more 'instant garden' is here to stay. Gardening has become more accessible than ever before with its mystique being broken down through television and other media. Although many of the makeover programmes may over-simplify gardening, they have encouraged many to see their outdoor space in a different light and helped them to consider how the garden may look and how it is likely to be used. People are unlikely to stay in one house for their entire lives and are too impatient to wait years before their garden looks good. Some plants are very slow growing and it can be infuriating to plant a garden and move property before they reach a reasonable size.

The city garden has become more closely connected to the interior spaces of a house or apartment, rather than 'blending in' with its surroundings, which used to be a major priority. In a way it has become more insular in that the garden is more likely to reflect some of the influences from the house, such as taking some of the materials or colours that are used inside and repeating them outside in the garden. Some gardens are so closely designed and linked to the interior that the transition between the two has become seamless and the garden has become a real 'indoor-outdoor' room.

When a house, apartment or office is being planned these days the garden is more likely to be integrated into the planning process rather than being an afterthought. With the advancement in communication systems, such as the Internet, there has been a rapid increase in people working from

home. Under these circumstances the garden can take on an important role and possibly be somewhere to add an extra indoor room by building an office or studio space. The journey to work for some may even become a walk through the garden. Likewise, due to advances in technology, communication and worldwide transportation, there are more plants and landscaping materials available than ever before. Combinations of these elements are being put together imaginatively to create exciting new compositions.

Tough modern materials such as coloured plastics, pre-fabricated paving materials, metals and fabrics are being used imaginatively by product and garden designers. Product designers are creating new ranges of accessories and furniture, which help to decorate the garden and introduce a wider variety of colours and textures into the composition.

Imaginative lighting will extend the hours the garden may be viewed from inside as well as increasing the hours it may be used into the evenings.

Above: **Traditional terracotta tiles are used in a contemporary way. The painted white wall reflects light into the shady space and the generous area of paving leaves the garden flexible for a variety of uses.**

Garden lighting can add real drama to even the simplest of gardens. Whether picking out a single sculptural plant with a hidden uplighter or imaginatively lighting a path for practical reasons, lighting can bring a garden to life. In the winter months, when it is dark early in the evenings and the garden is rarely used, imaginative lighting will bring a whole new dimension and turn it into a fantastic tonal composition to be viewed from inside. There are more types of lighting on the market than ever before and it is always worth considering lighting the garden at an early stage so as to plan any electrical work to be carried out.

There is no doubt that gardening can be one of the most creative of all pursuits. The blending of different textures, colours, sounds and scents to create a space with a uniquely distinctive feel is, no doubt, a true art form. This space is ever changing with the growing plants and the changing seasons, which help to keep the composition fresh. The new age of gardening has released the gardener and garden owner to be able to put in the time and interest at their own level – whether they want the garden to be a challenging and ongoing creative space or a simpler composition. Whatever level and style of garden you choose, see the garden as a room outside. A room to be lived in.

Child-friendly areas

Unfortunately, the city has become a more dangerous place for children and the garden has become the principal place for them to play. It seems that today's parents are much less likely to let their young

Opposite: **This garden combines a bold design with a simple formality, which is carried through in the evergreen structural planting of the box and cycad palms. It works effectively as a composition as well as being the perfect place to relax, entertain and swim.**

Below: **The garden in the city is a real bonus for all the family and has become the primary place for children to play safely. A child-friendly garden doesn't have to ruin the aesthetics of the design.**

Above: **Container gardening is, for many, the only way to grow plants in the city. These tall grasses help to break up the expanse of brick wall, and the simple repetition of the same large pots brings a designed look to a small space.**

children play away from the home for the fear that something may happen to them. For those with children and those who are planning to have children the garden has to be considered as a place to play safely. There are many ways in which the garden can be made safer. I don't believe in making a garden overly safe. A child can only learn from experience, but there is a difference between an educational garden and a downright dangerous one. It is almost impossible to oversee a small child every second of the day, let alone trying to relax yourself at the same time.

A garden to suit your needs

There are many people who would gladly spend all their spare time gardening – moving plants, propagating plants, and building new garden structures. These are the really keen gardeners who live and breathe gardening and see their gardens as either a major hobby or life-long adventure. At the other end of the scale is someone who has absolutely no interest or little time to carry out the actual gardening, for whatever reason, but does this mean they shouldn't have a successful garden? In between these two extremes there is a level of gardening for everyone. It is a simple calculation of interest, time, lifestyle, taste and income.

It is important to get the right level so that you can realistically achieve an aim and avoid the frustrations that many gardeners face. Many times have I seen people embark on garden projects without thinking the whole thing through, only to become unstuck half-way into the scheme for one reason or other and to end up with a half-finished garden. It is usually a case of lack of planning and more often than not a case of being over ambitious.

Garden making is usually divided into two main groups: hard landscaping and soft landscaping. The hard landscaping covers all the building work of a garden, such as paving, fencing, walling and pond building, and the soft landscaping is all the planting, topsoil and turfing or seeding of any lawn areas.

The planning process is very important and it is vital to get the hard landscaping right the first time as there is often a lot more heavy work involved in garden construction than, say, interior design. For example, the moving of large quantities of soil and the importing of sand, cement and bricks is expensive as well as time-consuming. A brick wall will have a foundation underground, which is not seen, but can throw up a lot of spoil. This spoil could be taken away off site or possibly used to change the levels within the garden. If the access to and from the garden is not very good – as is the case with so many city gardens – important decisions like this are worth considering early on.

If you are confident about designing your space yourself then that's fine, but if you have a tricky site or find the building aspect complicated then you could consider employing a garden designer. Why not? It may be that you have been looking at the same garden for a long time, and just can't see a way forward. A garden designer will at least see your garden with a fresh pair of eyes.

I employed an interior designer when my shop was being built as I just couldn't visualise the space. All his skills and knowledge of materials and costs resulted in me getting the best from my space: somewhere that functioned well, but was also aesthetically stimulating. He actually saved me money in the long run and I wouldn't think twice before employing an architect or designer again – even if it was simply on a consultancy basis for some inspiration.

Whichever way you decide to proceed with your garden I would say the most important things to bear in mind are to keep the scheme simple and be bold with the design. This is the basis for the exciting and contemporary garden designs that are currently being created in the modern city. *The Plant Room* explores contemporary city gardens from around the world, showing the wide range of gardens that are at the forefront of this new look, and the issues that confront the modern gardener.

Below: **Side alleys are common in the city and are often awkward spaces to deal with. The timber decking is deliberately laid lengthways to draw the eye to the water beyond.**

the versatile garden

As the garden is seen more and more as an outdoor room, it becomes a place where the whole family can relax, play and enjoy each other's company. What a bonus a garden in the city is for the whole family – somewhere to enjoy the good weather in the privacy and convenience of their own space without having to travel to a local park to experience the outdoors.

There is nothing better than going straight out into the garden on a beautiful sunny morning, starting off slowly with breakfast al fresco and then seeing how the day unfolds. The day may revolve completely around the garden without having to venture outside the home and its environs. Friends and family may pop over to enjoy the outside space and take the pressure off the parents by letting the children entertain each other.

The garden is becoming even more important for children as it is a safe place to play. These days, children are less likely to play in the streets or be allowed to go to the park without an adult. In the city, the levels of traffic considerably restrict the areas where children were once allowed to play. Within the perimeters of their own gardens, parents can keep an eye on their children and feel relaxed.

There is no reason why the design of a versatile garden should be particularly diluted. Once the way the space will be used and a general layout is set, the garden can be approached with the same exciting, contemporary and bold style as any other garden. The versatile garden needs to be designed with flexibility in mind as there will be a wide variety of demands put on to it. Interiors are now being designed in this way. Rather than sub-dividing a large interior space into smaller 'rooms' there is a movement towards larger single spaces, which can be used for a variety of purposes. These larger, airier open spaces lead to a more communal and interactive approach to family living and this multi-functional approach applies itself well to the garden, helping link the interior to the exterior rather than treating the garden as an add-on to the house.

Even though the city garden is far removed from a rural setting it is quite staggering how much variety and diversity of wildlife there is to be seen. The garden is often the place where a child first comes into contact with nature and starts to observe its surroundings. Although the garden can be quite safe it should never be a sterile place. It's important for children to come into contact with soil, insects and plants to develop their under-standing of how the world works. Ideally, plan an area into the garden – it may be as basic as a large pot – for a child to sow seeds and have a dig.

Of course a garden for the whole family can't be too precious a space. Inevitably plants will get trashed, but that's just the way it goes. It can be infuriating to have some plants that are flowering in all their glory ruined by a stray football or a child who doesn't stick to the paths, but on the other hand a garden that is solely designed for the children will become a playground. There are clever ways of designing gardens that can be both inviting to adults while still being a stimulating place for children without having to turn the whole garden into a theme park.

Previous pages: **The generous deck area makes this garden a highly flexible space for the whole family without turning the garden into a playground. The tall purple *Verbena bonariensis* in the foreground adds depth to the planting when repeated next to the hardy banana, *Musa basjoo*, towards the back.**

Layout

A versatile garden needs to work as a functional space and the success of the layout all depends on the balance between the functional and aesthetic values put on to the whole of the garden. A successful outdoor space works in a similar way to other rooms and meets the demands asked from it. For example, a well-planned kitchen will perfectly suit the way the owner cooks and uses the space as well as reflecting their personality and style at the same time. This leads to the owner feeling totally comfortable and at ease in their customised space. Ideally, this should apply to the garden too.

It is important with all garden layouts to try to maximise the use of the whole garden. There are too many gardens that have been designed with the terrace areas connecting straight on to the back of the house and a lawn area stuck on to that. As well as a design like this being visually flat when viewed from the house, it will do little to entice you into the garden. Try to visualise the garden in reverse and imagine what it would look like if you put the seating area towards the back of the garden. This may not be the right place, but it will help you to break the conventional approach to the layout.

The layout design can be initiated by a few simple decisions such as how many people you would like to get around a table to eat at any time or where to create a private space in the shade to read while the children are playing. Simple, generous layouts based on decisions like these will often work much better than trying hard to squeeze many separate areas out of a city garden, which will in effect leave fewer places that can realistically be used.

In my designs I try to give each garden at least one large space for general outdoor living. It is a common scenario for the garden owner to be initially concerned that the area is too large, but as soon as a table and a few chairs are placed on the surface it's amazing how the space will shrink. If there are too many people sitting on an area that is too small the whole experience can become quite disconcerting and it can feel a bit like you're stuck on a raft with no escape. If you entertain outside on a regular basis,

Above: **Be generous when building steps so they can be approached from a variety of angles. A single specimen such as this Mexican blue palm (*Brahea armata*) needs plenty of space around it so the whole of its form can be seen.**

design a garden where people come first as the plants and features are easier to adapt to a layout than the other way around.

It follows that with small gardens you should try to keep a consistent paving level throughout. This will help keep the majority of the space usable. If there is a level change or steps through the middle of a small garden it will lead to the space being considerably restricted in its use, as a table and chairs will have to either be on one level or the other.

'Plants and features are easier to adapt to a layout than the other way round'

Dividing the garden into two main areas to create separate spaces for the children to play and the older folk to relax in can work really well. Children love to be able to hide in a garden and have their own territory to mess about in. Screening off the back area with some trellising or taller planting can create a false end to a garden behind which the kids can play and keep the main area as a real garden. It's easy to leave breaks in the screen or have a low hedge so that the children can be seen if necessary.

I tend to try to incorporate interest for the children within the design of the main garden and encourage them to use the whole of the space rather than trying to keep them in their own areas. Try to imagine the garden as if you were a child. Paths and paved areas are better for riding trikes on than, say, gravel or bark areas. Low retaining walls become something to run along and jump off and therefore need some steps to be able to get up on to them easily. Simple water features or rills are perfect to sail toy boats down and a strong pergola becomes the perfect place to hang a swing or tyre for swinging on. A paddling pool needs a level surface, and will ruin a lawn underneath within a week.

In my own garden I have a paved area going right up to the wall without

Opposite: **Smooth rendered surfaces create the opportunity to add permanent colour into the garden. This yellow wall works well in summer, brightens up the garden in winter and intensifies the greens of the plants.**

a planting space in between. This has been done so that my son can kick a football against it and – who knows – possibly play for England one day! I've also made a movable shallow ramp, which can be simply placed against the steps so the kids can easily ride their bikes from one level to the next. Features such as these can easily be included into a design without ruining the aesthetics of the garden.

Shade

Some gardens can get incredibly hot and sunny. It is tempting to put the main terrace area in full sun, but in the heat of the summer it can be uncomfortable for both adults and children to sit in these areas without any

Below: **Hard surfaces are the most practical for the small garden. The small unit of a stable block is the perfect proportion for this garden. It also draws the eye through the strong layout whilst setting off the cool green of the plants.**

Above: **The roof structure will give shade from the sun as well as keep the area dry, and turns this garden into a real indoor/outdoor space that can be used all year round. The relaxing feel given by a garden surround creates the perfect place to entertain.**

shade. Temporary shades can easily be put up or down or a tree planted to give a cooling dappled shade. More permanent structures such as pergolas and gazebos can be built to create shade and will also give the opportunity to grow climbers and add instant height to a garden.

Surfaces

The lawn has generally been seen as the most appropriate family garden surface as it is soft, green and relatively cheap to install. But beware! A small lawn in a city garden more often than not just simply doesn't work, and it will considerably limit the amount of time a garden can be used. When wet it is uninviting and anyway a wet lawn should be kept off to avoid compaction. It can take a long time for a lawn to dry out after it has rained. The smaller the lawn the more work it will need as it will probably get more wear per square metre. Also, the shade and poor air circulation created by tall buildings and overhanging trees in an urban garden are not conducive to growing grass.

A lawn needs plenty of regular work to keep it in reasonable condition. On top of the regular mowing (at least once a week) it will need watering, feeding, scarifying and aerating. I love lying on a freshly mown lawn like everyone else, but the day I got rid of my small lawn was the day I could really start to enjoy and relax in my garden. My garden now gets used more than ever by all of us and I can concentrate my time on the areas of the garden I enjoy. If a lawn area is included in the design of your garden it is important that there is a way around the garden without stepping on the lawn. Otherwise, when it's wet, it will become a psychological and physical barrier between the house and what's beyond.

When making a choice about which surface to have there is very little difference between stone, brick, tiles or coloured concrete in as much as they are all a hard landing for a child who has fallen. They are all durable and practical surfaces for general use and are all low maintenance. Decking

Above: **An L-shaped retaining wall creates the perfect opportunity to build a seat with a back. It is a more efficient use of space than extra chairs as well as being an inviting place to sit.**

Opposite: **The cool colours and simple unfussy planting create a relaxing space for outdoor living. All the planting areas are mulched with cockleshells over a landscape fabric to minimize maintenance for the busy owners.**

is a slightly softer and quieter surface, which will also work well in a family garden. Gravel areas can introduce interesting textures and are easily planted through to soften the overall look, but pebbles are irresistible to young children and before long will be quickly scattered around the garden.

Safety

Safety is an important issue, especially where children are concerned. If the garden is a place to relax and unwind in, it has to also be a safe place where you don't have to be watching the children every minute of the day, and where you can be confident that the kids can't seriously injure themselves. Children are naturally inquisitive and will inevitably test a garden's safety to the max.

Water features such as ponds and pools are potentially the most dangerous element in a garden. It is a fact that babies can die in 5cm (2in) of water. We all know it's better to be safe than sorry and to make sure that if water is present in a garden that it is 100 per cent safe for small children to play nearby. Children do love the sense of play that water can bring to a garden, so see if there's a way of making the water feature safe before making a knee-jerk reaction to remove it altogether.

I removed the large pond in my garden when my children arrived as there was no way to make it both aesthetically pleasing and safe as it was such a dominant feature. Smaller ponds and water features can be made safe by fixing a heavy duty galvanised steel mesh at water level. If desired, large cobbles can be placed on the mesh to help improve the look.

Children love to climb on to low walls and run along them. Rather than attempt to discourage them it's easier all round to make the way up on to the wall easily accessible with some steps. This will help them both up and down and hopefully encourage them to use the same route and therefore cause less damage to the garden.

If you are planning to install a pre-fabricated climbing frame it is important to give children a soft landing when they fall. If you are giving

them the green light to get up high, then the chances are that they will fall at some time or other. Play bark or a lawn area is advisable and needs to be extremely generous all the way around the frame as children don't always fall straight down! The drawback of playbark is that it will inevitably get soggy, and will visually be rather dark and light-sapping. Features like climbing frames can end up really dominating a small garden, so consider carefully before buying one.

'The city garden therefore becomes a special place to both express ourselves and to interact with the immediate local community'

Community

Before putting up tall trellising or fences or growing a tall hedge to increase privacy think about your neighbours and how much contact or lack of contact you may want with them. For example, on one side of my garden there is a family with children of similar ages to ours. We all get on well and spend lots of time in our gardens together and chat over the low wall. We have intentionally kept the boundary low so that the children can easily climb over into each other's gardens and enjoy each other's company. On the other side I have grown a bamboo hedge to increase both our privacy and our neighbour's privacy from us, as that is what we have both agreed.

In an urban setting we all have to live side by side, but that is what city living is all about. We have to consider and tolerate each other, but at the same time do our own thing. The energy and vibrancy of the city encourage us to do this. We are much more likely to be both observed by and come into contact with our neighbours in our city gardens than we would inside our house or apartment. The city garden therefore becomes a special place to both express ourselves and to interact with the immediate local community.

Opposite left: **A great garden for young children that can be easily altered when they have grown up. The swing and sandpit could quickly be removed, and turned into planting areas.**

Opposite right: **This sandpit is designed as a future circular pond. It is a clever way of both completing the design with all the hard landscaping in place, whilst at the same time meeting the needs of the family.**

Plants

When choosing plants for a family-orientated garden it is important to select both sturdy and safe plants. Most plants are naturally robust. They may have their flowers damaged, which is always a shame, but they will generally bounce back and flower well next year. Most evergreen shrubs and bamboos are pretty tough, and can take the occasional bashing. Tall perennials are the most likely to get damaged as one stray ball can quickly ruin a swathe of colourful flowers such as delphiniums or the taller poppies. Lower growing perennials like hardy geraniums and *Alchemilla mollis* are a better bet as they can take the occasional trampling, and will spread reasonably quickly anyway.

As far as safety with plants is concerned I'm a firm believer in learning through play, and there are some plants that can quickly become 'educational' without being too dangerous. Once they have been experienced it's likely they will be kept well clear of next time around. These are plants with small thorns or spiky leaves such as eryngiums or most of the roses. On the other hand, plants with large spikes such as pyracantha or the yuccas can be seriously dangerous to children, and even adults. The eye-level of anyone who may be in the garden should be considered carefully, and it is best to avoid planting these plants or to take them out if they are inherited with the garden.

The real dangers in the garden, however, come from the plants that are either poisonous or a skin irritant. A young child can't distinguish between an edible berry, such as a blackberry or blackcurrant, and the poisonous berries of deadly nightshade or the pods of a laburnum tree. They all look tasty to them. Indeed, some of the most attractive garden plants can cause serious skin problems and even permanent scarring. Euphorbias have a milky white sap that is a powerful irritant, and all the parts of the oleander – especially the sap – are toxic. It's best to walk around the garden with a list of dangerous plants (see pages 160–1) and see exactly what you have in your garden and assess the real dangers before letting your children loose.

Opposite: **The steel blue concrete is a hard-wearing surface and visually sets off the deck and planting areas effectively. The main seating area has been designed into the centre of the garden to increase privacy from overlooking neighbours, and it ensures that the whole of the garden space available is fully used.**

the front garden

The front garden of a city house has to be designed to meet many different criteria while at the same time making a simple statement about you, the homeowner. A front garden in a city is a very personal thing as it identifies you to all the passers-by. In most roads in a cosmopolitan city there is plenty of traffic, whether on foot, bicycle, car or bus, who will all be looking into your front garden. In fact, this space is almost public visual property and will be seen by many more people than would see any of your other outdoor or indoor spaces. The front garden is an area that is unlikely to be used for outdoor living. It therefore becomes somewhere to create a strong and simple visual composition.

An important factor when designing a front garden is how it may look with regard to the rest of the street, and this is where the personality of the homeowner and the particular kind of statement they would like to make comes into play. Many people attempt to blend in with their surroundings as much as possible so as not to draw attention to themselves. Their inspiration may come

Above: **The front garden can be the perfect place to experiment with planting, and create something special that will make a statement about yourself to all passers-by.**

Previous pages: **The size of the glass panels has been used to define the width of the stone path. Natural stone will help to anchor a building to the ground, whilst the birch trees keep the composition light.**

from looking at their neighbours' gardens and then merging their front gardens into the street by using similar materials and plants. Its setting, therefore, goes beyond the boundaries of the property and becomes part of the image of the whole street. If the majority of the front gardens in a particular road all use plants and materials along the same lines you may decide that to use anything too different may ruin the effect as a whole. The materials therefore may have already been decided, but that doesn't mean you can't create an interesting and designed look in your own front garden.

The front garden can alternatively be the place to let loose and express yourself. The degree of statement all depends on what you want to say. It can become the ideal canvas on which to show the whole world how much of an eccentric individual you are, and how creative you may be.

As a child I lived in a street where our next door neighbour used his front garden to exhibit his painted junk metal sculptures to the world (it was the early 70s!). It is the only front garden in the road that sticks in my mind and I know it gave great pleasure to many passers-by. To do something like this is a daring step to take and the general public will judge you on it, but if executed well the front garden can be the perfect place to introduce a sense of play and humour to the city.

Layout

The front garden also has the important job of visually connecting the building to the ground. There are usually several practical issues to plan around such as bin stores, degrees of privacy, car parking, ease of route to the front door and security.

A front garden should first and foremost relate to the building it sits in front of. This does not necessarily mean that it should appear to have been built or planted to match exactly the same period of the house, but it has to work with the building even if it has a much more modern and contemporary feel than the house. The front garden needs to help the property sit in its setting – almost anchor it to the ground. If the house is of a large imposing nature it will need a substantial design to complement it. If it has strong geometric lines or an uncompromising symmetry then the front garden should reflect this. Look for details such as window placement in the building that can be incorporated into the layout of the garden.

Modern buildings are often based on sleeker and more linear proportions. It therefore follows that it is generally easier to create a modern look in the front garden as the materials of the house will be of a more contemporary nature. Furthermore, it is less likely that there will be a particular historical period that the design needs to be sensitive to. Taking the design of the front elevation of the house and laying it as if it were in plan on to the garden will really help to introduce the building's proportions into the landscape.

Often the front gate will line up with the front door, but if the garden is large enough and symmetry isn't essential to the design it's worth considering diagonally off-setting the two so the whole of the garden is used to walk through. On the other hand, if the walk is made too long it can be a drawback if carrying shopping or pushing children's buggies.

Be generous with paths and consider paving a majority of the area. The path should follow the route that is most commonly used and should be easy to walk up rather than feeling like you may fall off it. This may sound obvious, but remember that if it is too thin or meanders too much there will be a temptation to short cut it, which will lead to plants getting damaged as a front garden will get plenty of pedestrian traffic.

To achieve a contemporary look in a front garden it is best to stick to clean lines and to avoid fussy

Below: **This garden is split into two areas, one for off-street parking and the other as a planting composition. The red maple in the pot makes a great focal point.**

33

Opposite: **The front of a house creates the perfect opportunity to grow a climber such as this fantastic wisteria. The simple planting uses a few single specimens to create a strong, but welcoming, entrance.**

shapes. Simple bold formality can work extremely well when designing front gardens. This can be achieved through the combined layout and planting. When designing the layout for a front garden it's best to have an idea of plants you want to use so you can create particular spaces for them in the hard landscaping. If you want to plant a climber up the front of the building or have, say, two box balls either side of the front entrance make sure the paving is laid accordingly. Otherwise you will need to plant everything in planters, which may detract from the composition as a whole and increase maintenance through watering.

Landscaping materials

The landscaping materials of a front garden have to be very carefully considered. The material of the building and the way the garden surface may work alongside it is absolutely crucial to the overall success of the composition. It is often better to look for a complementary material rather than attempting to copy the material of the building itself. If a house is made of red brick it can be overwhelming to use the same material in the front garden. The result can be a rather municipal looking space rather than an inviting front garden.

'The subtlety of more neutral and natural materials such as stone, slate or granite all give a feeling of solidity and permanence'

The paving material should ideally be of heavier substance than the building itself. A lightweight material such as decking against a brick or stone building may not have quite enough visual weight to tie down the building. The subtlety of more neutral and natural materials such as stone, slate or granite all give a feeling of solidity and permanence, which helps to

connect a building to the ground without attempting to grab the eye. They are also extremely hard wearing, which is important as the front entrance to a house will get more wear than any other part of the exterior landscape. Using the same landscape materials can help to connect the front and back gardens.

If there is a side alley or space to wrap a continuous paving around the building from the front to back gardens it will give the effect of a more cohesive space and lead to a designed look. It will also help the entire building to sit comfortably in its setting.

For strong visual impact limit yourself to no more than two surface materials. Small unit paving materials such as brick or tiles can be laid in a variety of ways. A linear format, avoiding random patterns, or occasional inserts usually looks best in a front garden. Small units of paving can also be laid to create direction in paving. If bricks are laid lengthways towards the door from the gate it will draw the eye quickly towards the door. In contrast, if laid horizontally across the field of view it will slow down the eye and increase the apparent width of a path.

Boundaries

Again with the boundaries it is better to either go with the exact period of the house or be sympathetic with the structure and do something more contemporary that works well and helps to complement it. Contrary to the paving materials it usually works well to match the brick or particular finish of the house when creating verticals such as boundary walls. The height of any boundaries should ideally work with the proportions of the house, so if it is a low-level house use a low-level fence or wall and a taller boundary for a taller building.

Below: **Throw the textbook out of the window and get creative. This imaginative fence made from reclaimed materials and wild-style planting makes an intriguing contrast to the house beyond.**

Privacy can usually be increased with boundaries such as walls, fences, railings, hedges and trellising. They will vary or can be custom made to be as solid or as see through as you would like. Walk along the road and see where you would like to increase privacy and remember it's the eye-level of a tall person that is the crucial aspect, and the height of the boundary in relation to that eye-level. If the street level is higher than the windows you want to obscure you may not need as tall a wall or fence as you thought. Tall boundaries will inevitably increase the shade, so the relationship between the solidity and height of a boundary will affect both the privacy and shade created by the structure.

Planting

To achieve a clean and contemporary look in a front garden the planting needs to be planned accordingly. The particular criteria applied to meet the demands of the plants should help in the selection process. Plants need to be chosen for specific qualities such as height, leaf shape and colour and whether they are evergreen or not. The planting will also depend on the aspect of the garden – whether it is sunny or shady, or somewhere in between. Structural planting such as hedging and large shrubs are exactly what hold a front garden together and give it the solidity with the hard landscaping to help tie the building to the ground.

Box is an invaluable plant to use as structural planting to any garden. It is relatively low maintenance, needing only the occasional trim and feed. Hedges help with both structure and privacy. With a small front garden look mainly for plants with height, but without too much spread as otherwise they will take up too much space. This will probably be achieved through clipping the hedge to keep its shape. Yew or *Thuja plicata* can be kept clipped to any shape to form a solid and formal hedge. *Cotoneaster lacteus* or *Choisya ternata* can be cut back to create the right height without too much spread and either will give a more informal feel as a hedge for a front

Above: **Simple formality sometimes just can't be beaten. These tall elegant planters planted with box balls have been custom made for the site. They are just the right proportion and look perfect for the entrance to this house.**

garden. *Phoenix canariensis* will give a more exotic feel and as it has a vase shape to it will help to create privacy at the right height when planted in quantity. The taller bamboos make great hedges as they give height, don't need any clipping or get too dense.

There is often the chance in a front garden to plant a single small tree, which can add height and interest. One of the many *Acer palmatum* varieties can look fantastic as a single specimen and give the most stunning display of autumn foliage. If the climate is kind enough consider a standard olive tree. They have a beautiful silvery leaf, keep small and are evergreen. In colder areas, the willow-leaved pear *Pyrus salicifolia* will achieve a similar look, but it is a deciduous tree and will therefore lose its leaves, and look twiggy throughout the winter

The front garden is the perfect place to plant some of the highly scented winter and early spring flowering plants. In a back garden they can easily be missed at this time of year as it is unlikely you will spend time outside in the cold, but in the front garden the fragrance cannot be ignored as you walk past them. *Osmanthus* x *burkwoodii* forms a neat, dense evergreen mound and has highly scented white tubular flowers in early spring. Its domed shape can help strengthen the structural planting. *Sarcococca confusa* is one of the most highly scented early flowering plants with its clusters of cream flowers in late winter. The daphnes all have remarkably strong scented flowers in late winter to mid-summer and are a real treat to pass by.

Lighting

If you decide to light your front garden remember that you are immediately making a statement about yourself to the passers-by. Subtlety is the key with all forms of lighting so try to use low wattage bulbs and fittings. If you have a single tree or large specimen shrub in a small front garden it can often be enough lighting for the whole garden to throw up a single uplighter into the crown. Consider, too, the practical aspect of lighting paths with

Opposite: **The planting of clipped box, yew and white impatiens combined with the brick and stone paving gives weight and solidity to this front garden.**

low-level footlighter type fittings to help guide you to the front door. Lighting near the front door will also help when trying to put the key in the lock when it's dark. Both these forms of lighting help to increase the security of a property.

Low-level lighting to accent any symmetrical planting either side of the front door or along the walls of the house can look really effective and adds form to the imposing nature of a well-designed entrance. But avoid lighting the house itself. Unless the building is stunning enough, throwing light on to house walls at night is generally tacky and ostentatious. The glare of the lights will be distracting from inside, and do you really want to be the only house in the street that lights up at night?

Maintenance

As a front garden has to be the ultimate in low maintenance – being pretty much as maintenance-free as a garden gets – it is worth planning the garden so as not to have any bare soil areas, which will encourage weeds. Landscaping fabrics are worth their weight in gold here. These fabrics are a semi-permeable membrane, which will let water through whilst being a physical barrier to suppress any weeds. They can be placed directly on the soil and pinned down with pegs. Holes are easily cut in the fabric to plant through and then any kind of mulch such as pebbles or crushed shells can be placed on top to a depth of about 5cm (2in). This mulch also helps retain moisture in the soil while keeping the weeds out. Light-coloured mulches such as pebbles, gravel or crushed shells will really help to brighten up an area and set the plants off better than any bare soil, which is dark and will therefore sap the natural light. Larger, 20mm (¾in) pebbles are better than too fine a grade. They will not be used by neighbouring cats as litter and won't get caught in the tread of shoes, which can lead to them being trodden into the house.

Opposite: **The strong architecture of this modern building with its generous steps needs a sympathetic front garden. There is plenty of space to make a wide, welcoming entrance and an additional seating area to catch the evening sun.**

the roof
garden

The roof garden can be a truly unique and exhilarating space from which the vibrancy of urban life can be viewed, taken part in – or escaped from. In a strange way, sometimes all at the same time. Roof gardens brilliantly demonstrate the city dwellers' need to create a garden, however uninviting the initial environment. As designers and gardeners alike find innovative ways of exploiting all outdoor spaces connected with a building, so the roof garden has benefited tremendously from the increasing interest in gardening. Roof gardens are now often seen as being equal in importance and potential to a more conventional type of garden space and have become just as much a priority for many when buying or renting property as a garden. However small, the outdoor space can give a property an all-important feeling of freedom – creating an oasis in the city.

For these reasons, roof gardens are more and more frequently being given priority at preliminary stages of residential developments and integrated into modern, purpose-built apartments or created as add-ons to existing houses. Initially, the roof space is a difficult place to create a garden. There are usually more practical and safety issues to consider than would be the case in a more conventional garden but, with careful planning, the sky is literally the limit.

Each unique city skyline, which is often dominated by tall buildings and landmarks, can be totally detached from a naturalistic or rural backdrop. This strange freedom invites the gardener to let their imagination run riot to create a garden of their dreams. The roof garden will test the ingenuity and imagination of the city dweller to the maximum in transforming an often hostile environment into a space that can be both inviting and thrilling. The mere idea of having a garden in the sky would not exist without the buildings found within a city and it is a reflection of gardeners' resourcefulness to garden upwards when they cannot spread themselves laterally any more.

A stunning roof-top garden may contain an element of surprise, catching the unsuspecting visitor completely unaware. The basic idea of the garden can be elevated to a secret floating fantasy world. The added privacy a roof garden may bring, when combined with a sweeping city view, can often uncover the hidden beauty an urban landscape may hold. In the summer evenings the cityscape comes alive and there is nowhere better to view it from than up high among the rooftops. The proportions of a roof garden are usually based directly on the proportions of the interior rooms and therefore work very well when linking together the two spaces.

Planning and layout

The planning of a roof garden is often more important for a variety of reasons and therefore it is essential to have a very strong idea of what you want and have a definite plan to work towards. This will help to avoid any extra unnecessary work and it will also help you to attain a garden that you are happy with and proud of. For example, there are more practical issues, which need to be dealt with when constructing a roof terrace, compared to

Above: **Roof gardens demonstrate the city dweller's need to create a garden. This roof garden overlooks a courtyard garden whilst cleverly connecting the rooms together at first-floor level.**

Previous pages: **The trellising increases privacy whilst echoing the sleek clean lines of the decking to create a cohesive and designed look to the roof garden. Simple canvas sails make the perfect shades, and complete the simple design.**

an average back garden at ground level. Weight and wind are the most important as safety must come first. It is advisable to consult a structural engineer when converting a roof space into a garden. They will advise you about any planning requirements, weight loads and safety regulations that are particular to the existing site.

Roof gardens can be problematic to set up initially, as there is usually a lot of carrying work involved. Access can often be very restricted and it is sometimes worth the careful planning of having a lot of the bulky things delivered at the same time and hiring a winch to raise them up the outside of the building. Safety is a very important issue for you, but for the general public and insurance it is essential. So consider employing a local contractor to undertake this work.

The approach to the roof garden will affect the layout of the space immensely. If the roof space is hidden from any of the house or apartment rooms and is accessed solely by climbing a flight of stairs, then the layout and composition don't necessarily have to tie in with or relate directly to the rooms in the house. The garden becomes almost isolated and the design can be approached as a separate item to the interior. The visual terms of reference may be taken from the extended landscape. A way to extend the view is to implement a technique called 'framing the view', which manipulates the direction the eye will be drawn by the strategic placing of plants or boundaries. Some cityscapes are breathtaking and should be left open and not obscured. Another simple way to link the garden with the view beyond is to mimic clay chimney pots by placing planted terracotta pots on the walls (but make sure they are securely fixed!).

If the views beyond are unattractive or if privacy from overlooking apartments is an issue, consider erecting strong visual boundaries. But remember that if boundaries are put up on all the perimeters they will retain all the interest within the garden and it will feel detached from any existing setting.

If the garden is closely linked to a main room in the house then the

Below: **This tiny balcony garden is only 3 metres by 2 metres. Many of the plants are supported by a cantilevered shelf hanging on the outside of the wall, and the parasol doubles in the rain as an umbrella.**

whole layout and composition has to be considered in relation to the interior. If there are large windows or sliding doors the garden room will be usable throughout the summer and a real inside-outside space is achievable. If the garden is to be viewed all of the year from inside, then a solid composition will carry it through. Often the most obvious place to have a seating area is right next to the doors that lead from the house. This is often the case in conventional gardens where the terrace or patio is placed right next to the house. It is sometimes an overly simplistic approach to the use of the space. The space next to the garden entrance is often better left uncluttered so as to draw you into the whole garden space.

Consider the city views, the way the sun works around the sky, the privacy and the way you'd like to use the whole space. Are you a sun lover or do you like to sit in the shade? Do you want to maximise the space to fit eight people around a table for a dinner party? These are the sorts of questions that should be asked before considering what are your favourite 'must have' plants.

Surfaces

The choice of surface is usually the first issue to address when converting a roof into a garden space. There is a wide range of materials suitable for the roof garden, which will create the look you are seeking. Many flat-roof areas start off with a black asphalt surface, which can be both visually and practically hostile. In the heat of the summer this type of surface can become unbearably hot. The heat will also make the asphalt soft and often too soft for any practical use. This membrane must not be punctured as it is sealed and water tight and sometimes means that furniture and pots can't be placed on the surface.

Timber decking is probably the most commonly used surface for a roof garden. Although it has been criticised as a passing fad, I think it is a classic surface with many good qualities, which make it hard to overlook.

Opposite left: **For some a roof garden or balcony is all they would want for an outside space. Timber decking is the most commonly used surface as it is light and easy to install.**

Opposite right: **A stunning rooftop garden contains an element of surprise to the visitor. It will test the ingenuity of the city dweller to turn a hostile environment into a space that is both inviting and thrilling.**

There is no doubt it is an attractive finish and can give the effect of an interior wooden floor and therefore increase the feeling of taking the indoors outside to create a room. The simple clean lines of a deck will certainly add a contemporary feel to any garden. It can also conjure up images of boat holidays or coastal destinations, which can help you to escape from the city. As far as installation is concerned, decking is a very easy and relatively cost-efficient surface to put down. A long-lasting and attractive hardwood, such as iroko, is the ideal timber to use although it can get expensive. The pressure treated softwoods now come with a very long rot-proof guarantee and are very good value for money.

Timber is a relatively light material, which means that it can be carried to the roof easily and will not add too much to the overall weight of the roof. In fact, once installed, it will actually help to spread the weight of people, pots, plants and furniture across the whole of the roof. Timber is also a clean material to work with and doesn't require any cement work. The decked roof can also help to reduce noise if there is a room underneath, as well as helping soak up sound when on the roof itself. Timber decking is a relatively soft material compared to stone or brick and therefore is ideal for children to play on. If it is in the shade it may become slippery and benefit from an annual pressure wash to remove any residue.

Although decking is a good choice there are other materials worth considering, which can work very well as a surface for the roof terrace. Synthetic grass can look extremely effective and instantly green-up an area. I find it uncomfortable to sit on but it can be used in areas of the roof garden that are to be viewed rather than sat in. It can also contrast well with decking and different gravels. A thin decorative dressing of gravel or rounded pebbles can help to cover the unattractive asphalt surface. Make sure to put down a membrane between the pebbles and the asphalt so that they don't sink in when the surface becomes soft. Additionally, thin tiles such as slate or sandstone can be laid on top of a waterproof surface often

without adding too much weight and work very well when extending the feel of the interior on to the roof terrace.

Weight

Weight is probably the most important practical issue to consider when planning a roof garden. Plants, soil and pots all add to the weight considerably and don't forget that when the soil is wet it will increase the total weight even more. To help distribute the weight of a deck, consider fixing it into any parapet walls around the edge. Planters, too, can often be fixed into these side walls by using brackets so that these side walls are actually taking the weight rather than the roof surface. Shelving systems running along these walls can also work well as they can help to raise the level of the planting for the visual impact as well as helping to take the weight off the roof.

Wind

One of the main issues to deal with at an early stage is the exposure to strong winds. There are many plants that cannot tolerate constant bombardment by the wind and will constantly be struggling to survive, let alone look good. Even in summer the wind can be strong and it can restrict the times the roof garden can be used. No one really enjoys being buffeted constantly by the wind and so it is important to try to create shelter. Windbreaks can deal with a variety of issues in one go. They can reduce the strength of the wind, which in turn creates a more favourable environment for a wider variety of plants. They can also deal with the common problem

Left: **Roof gardens are often exposed to strong winds and sun. As well as keeping the midday sun off this seating area, a bamboo shade makes an interesting composition with the** shadows it casts. Here decking is used to make the seat as well as the flooring surface. It is a practical choice, and adds a contemporary feel to the overall design.

of privacy on a roof garden by being a visual screen as well. It may not be possible to create a windbreak all the way around the roof terrace so plan an area where you may want to sit before doing any work.

A solid barrier, such as a brick wall or fence, can often have the reverse effect it is meant to have as far as creating a windbreak is concerned. The wind will be forced up and over the barrier and will often add to the problem rather than reduce it as it may create strong eddies on the garden side. It is a better idea to filter the wind by creating a partial screen such as a trellis or hedge. Container-grown hedges work very well in a roof garden as a wind filter as well as helping to formalise a space. If there is enough room, they can divide the space into two therefore creating two outdoor rooms. Good plants to grow as a windbreak include bamboo, *Thuja plicata* and yew.

Shade

In the summer, it is important that the roof garden has areas to sit in that are shaded from the heat of the sun. The combination of wind and strong sun can be misleading and can easily lead to sunburn, especially with children. Shade can be created in many ways. Strategic placing of a pot-grown tree or combination of trees such as the false acacia (*Robinia pseudoacacia* 'Frisia') will give a cooling dappled shade. Structures, such as pergolas or gazebos, will help to shade the sun as well as creating the opportunity to grow scented climbers such as honeysuckle and jasmine. Canvas works very well as a shade and is probably the most flexible as it can be put up and taken down as necessary. Canvas sun umbrellas are commonly available with stands and come in a variety of colours, shapes and sizes. Canvas sheeting can also be custom made to span a specific area and can be hung on hooks or run along yachting cable on a series of sewn-in rings. This will also give the roof garden a boat feel, which links in well with a timber deck.

Opposite: **Small trees such as this silver birch can help to give instant impact and added height to the planting, which can be difficult to achieve when planting in containers on a roof garden.**

Pots and planters

There is a wide variety of planters available and some of them are made of a lightweight material suitable for use on a roof garden. To achieve a contemporary look in a roof garden it is important to choose a single finish of planter and stick to it. There may be the opportunity to contrast the main type of planter with another when used as a focal point, but as a general rule it is important to be disciplined and restrained. A mish-mash of pots, which vary in colour, texture, size and shape, will instantly make any garden look untidy.

'Geometric cubed, rectangular or cylindrical shaped planters will keep the overall look clean and stylish'

These days there are plenty of types of pots and planters to choose from, which would give a contemporary look to a roof garden. Fibreglass, plastic, galvanised steel and wooden planters are all lightweight and widely available. It's best to try to stick to simple shapes. Single containers or combinations of containers can also be made to measure so as to fit a certain space within the roof garden. Simple painted or stained timber boxes made from a waterproof plywood are lightweight and add the opportunity of introducing colour into the garden. They could also be clad with copper sheeting or a textured metal finish to add an original and modern feel. Geometric cubed, rectangular or cylindrical shaped planters will keep the overall look clean and stylish.

The heavier planters such as stone or terracotta can be used if the roof structure is built to withstand heavy weights. Simple wooden trays with wheels or castors are worth thinking about for the heavier planters. The planters can be placed on them and then moved with ease, thereby increasing the flexibility of the space.

Planting

Contrary to popular belief there is a huge range of plants that can be grown in containers. After all, we buy most of our plants from the nursery or garden centre, which have lived their entire lives in pots. As long as each plant is given the right conditions and has the light, water and food it needs it should be perfectly happy.

All the plants on a roof garden will probably have to be grown in containers and therefore for every plant you will need a pot to grow it in. As a plant will inevitably outgrow its pot, either the plant (if it's a shrub or tree) or the pot will have to be replaced. This is an important consideration and it is important to give a container-grown plant room to grow. It is

Below left: **With modern buildings the roof garden is often incorporated into the initial architecture, and is likely to be able to take more weight. Larger planters can therefore be custom-built to fit the space.**

Below right: **There is nowhere better to view the cityscape than from high amongst the rooftops. It is a reflection of our resourcefulness to garden upwards when we cannot spread ourselves laterally any more.**

Above: **A roof garden designed to be used all the time – it even has its own kitchen area! The red flowering oleander in the foreground enjoys the protection of the wall.**

Previous pages: **Here there is a hint of East meets West. The city garden becomes the place to fuse different styles so that it sits comfortably in the metropolis whilst reflecting urban culture.**

beneficial to have the luxury and immediate impact of buying a few larger specimens, which will give a roof garden an instant look, but do make sure there is enough room in the pots for these larger specimens to grow. Spare space is often limited on a roof garden and a surplus of varying sized pots to pot on plants is not always possible.

If you can see the roof garden all year round it is important to have a good evergreen planting structure. If using hedging as a windbreak this will help to create a strong structure. If the garden is not visible from within the house then it is not so important to carry the interest all through the year as it probably won't be used during the winter months.

The plants should be approached in a similar way to the planters. The planting will give a much more designed look if you limit the variety of plants and think about the rhythm of the planting and how it will read as a sequence rather than focusing on each individual plant. The repetition of simple planting, such as a line of lavender or rosemary, is much more effective than an array of various heights and colours.

Bold and large-leaved plants, such as fig trees or fatsias, will have the effect of visually drawing the space inwards and keeping the focus within the roof terrace. More feathery-leaved plants, such as tamarisks or santolinas, have the opposite effect of increasing the space and blurring the boundaries of a roof garden, which can make the space feel larger.

Think about the placing of the largest plants first. Small trees can give instant impact and height, which is often lacking in the planting of roof terraces. A cleverly placed single tree can sometimes help to create enough privacy from overlooking windows. Mediterranean and coastal plants such as *Cordyline australis* and *Trachycarpus fortunei* will both add height and work well on roof terraces as they can tolerate exposure to sun and strong winds. Olive trees with their silvery evergreen foliage are superb pot-grown trees and can tolerate colder conditions than you may expect.

'Think about the rhythm of the planting and how it will read as a sequence rather than focusing on each individual plant'

Large shrubs such as *Arbutus unedo* or *Pittosporum tenuifolium*, can be used to create a windbreak or be planted as individual specimens as they cope well with the exposed conditions. Whether planted as single specimens or used as an informal hedge, both can be pruned to shape as necessary. Flowering shrubs, such as the silver-leaved cistus and *Convolvulus cneorum*, all work very well on a sunny roof terrace as do rosemary and lavender, whose scented foliage is unmistakable. It is important to ensure that if it is the flower of the plant that is scented that it flowers during a period when the roof garden will be in use. Many of the scented flowering shrubs flower early in the year and would be missed if the garden were not being used.

Many of the ornamental grasses will thrive on a roof garden as they like sunny open sites and the well-drained conditions of containers. The silver-leaved grasses, such as *Helictotrichon sempervivens* and the smaller *Festuca glauca*, will bring delicate new textures to the planting. The form of grasses often complements containers really well as they will droop gently over the edges. The late-summer seed heads will take the composition through into winter. Perennial plants grown in pots, which are usually divided approximately every three years, can be lifted, divided and re-potted in the usual way and therefore can be maintained at a desired size.

As the plants will be grown in imported soil it means that a variety of plants can be grown regardless of the acidity of the soil. For example, if you want to grow acid-loving plants like camellias and skimmias they can be planted into pots with ericaceous compost and grown alongside plants that thrive in a more alkaline soil.

Furniture

Space and storage are two issues to consider when buying furniture for the roof garden. Will the furniture need to stay out all winter? Can it fold up and be put to one side if necessary?

Built-in seating is well worth considering during the

planning stages of a roof terrace. Built-in seats will help to maximise the often limited space as well as side stepping the issue of furniture storage during the winter months. Simple bench seating made from timber, which runs along a wall, can cleverly double up as a shelf for pots and plants. If the seating is fixed into a house wall a good back is made for the seat. The addition of some cushions brought from inside will help to decorate the space as well as making the seats more comfortable.

Lightweight aluminium and fabric fold-up chairs and tables can be easily stored and are now widely available. The canvas or polyester fabrics are available in a range of colours, which can be a good way of introducing colour into the roof terrace. Painting walls the same or a complementary colour to furniture can be very effective and help the furniture to sit well in the space. Stick to one style and colour of chair for a cohesive and designed look.

Lighting

Both practical and decorative lighting can help to bring a roof garden to life in the evenings. During the summer months electric lighting can be both practical and decorative and sometimes both. The practical aspect of roof-terrace lighting includes lighting any hazards, such as changes in levels, spiral staircases and corners of buildings, as well as pooling light on to a dining table for evening meals. The decorative side can be highly creative and incorporate different techniques to create various effects (see 'The Night Garden'). Uplighters on spikes can be placed into the larger pots to create some dramatic images.

If it can be viewed from inside, creative lighting can turn a roof garden into a beautiful composition during the frosty winter months. Lighting is worth considering early on as any electrical work undertaken may need to be done prior to the construction work. If a timber deck is being installed it is likely that the cables can run underneath the slats to where the fittings are going to be placed. Light fittings can easily be recessed into decking to wash light on to adjacent walls or planters.

Irrigation

Irrigation is extremely important in the roof garden if the aim is to reduce maintenance as well as to keep the plants looking healthy all year round. Plants in containers dry out much more quickly than if they are planted directly into the ground. The wind found on most roof terraces will increase the speed at which these planters dry out and therefore regular watering is essential. Watering by hand with a watering can is a slow process and if there is only an indoor tap it will require plenty of trips. Even if there is a hosepipe available it still takes time to walk round making sure all the plants are watered. Instead, a drip irrigation system can ensure that all the plants will get the required quantities of water and if the system is put on to a small computer the system will turn itself on and off to a pre-set timer. The plumbing in of an outside water outlet will save weeks of watering over the years.

Water-retaining crystals, which are mixed into the soil when planting and swell by absorbing water, will significantly help to stop pots drying out. They are well worth considering if an irrigation system is not going to be installed. Be careful not to add them if an irrigation system is also installed as it may lead to water logging.

Maintenance

For some, a roof garden is all they would ever want for a garden. There is often little gardening to do in the conventional sense (as far as mowing, digging and weeding goes) and, in fact, when getting started, it is more of an installation. This leaves the gardener in total control of their space and allows them to spend as much or as little time gardening as they wish.

Page 58: **A green oasis in the sky. The roof garden – however small – can be the perfect antidote to busy city living.**

Page 59: **Modern buildings are more likely to consider the inclusion of a roof garden at an early stage of design as it is an efficient use of space. Movable furniture keeps this space more flexible for a variety of uses.**

Opposite: **A pergola construction provides essential shade for a roof garden. It also creates the opportunity to grow a grapevine and Virginia creeper to add height to the planting.**

As an ongoing process, the regular feeding of plants is crucial as they are probably pot grown or planted in raised planters. The nutrients quickly leach out of the soil and therefore feeding is more important than when a plant is planted directly into the ground.

The re-potting of plants is probably the biggest job to undertake on a roof garden. Every plant will eventually outgrow its container and, to keep it looking healthy, will need room for its roots to spread. Make sure that you use new compost and soil as the old blend will probably be exhausted.

the backyard, alley and basement well

For a number of reasons, many city dwellers have only small, sometimes awkward, areas of outside space available to them. For example, a backyard, alley or basement well. The division of the majority of city houses into apartments often leads to the garden spaces being squeezed into the size of a postage stamp. An estate agent might call this area 'petite' or 'cosy', but the truth is that there is little to work with.

The small backyard was the place to hang the washing or shake the dust from the rugs. On a summer's day it may have become the place to peel the potatoes or for children to play, but it was rarely thought of as a real garden, somewhere to relax or invite friends round for a drink.

Terraced houses often had side alleys designed into the property to let light into more of the rooms. In a semi-detached house these side alleys would frequently run alongside the whole

Previous pages: **This strong contemporary composition relies on simple geometric shapes being put together with thought and style. The structural elements of glass, stone, metal and wood are set off by the orange wall and architectural plants.**

Below: **The simple contrast in the foliage shapes of the trachycarpus, zantedeschia and acer is easily read against the white painted wall, which also helps to bounce light into the backyard.**

property and connect the rear garden to the front of the house. This would not only let light into more rooms but also provide good access to the garden from the road.

Basement wells, whether they are at the front or rear of the property, are usually designed to maximise natural light and access into the lower ground floors. The initial building work would be made easier with the access to the basement floors. The coal or wood storage areas were designed into the front basement areas for easy delivery access.

These are the areas that are now viewed and valued in a different way and seen as a bonus to any property we live in, whether rented or bought. However awkward, with some careful planning and imagination, almost any outside space can be transformed into somewhere that is pleasant to be in, and a critical addition to any garden. We just have to accept the size limitations and go forward positively. When designing awkward spaces such as these all the tricks are needed to maximise the feeling of space and increase the amount of light let into these areas. The choice of flooring, walls, planting and lighting all need to be considered carefully to keep the final composition as airy and light as possible. The manipulation of the space needs to be carried out both boldly and confidently to achieve an often-permanent composition.

Layout

The biggest consideration when designing the layout of a backyard, side alley or basement well is what can the space be realistically used for? Will you be able to sit in it? Will you have to store things in it as well? If this area is the only outdoor space you have, then you may well want to keep it as flexible as possible for a variety of uses. However, it is important to decide on its central function when it comes to conceiving the layout, as putting too many demands on one small space may well end up with you failing to make it work for anything really effectively. It is also important to remember that many of these areas can be viewed from inside the house, and therefore the layout should take into account the ways in which it may be an aesthetic extension of an interior.

The spaces discussed in this chapter are usually dominated by shade, so the consideration of where to place a seating area may not need to be dictated by the movement of the sun. However, considerations such as whether or not a door will open outwards into the area will profoundly affect the layout of the space.

If the main aim is to maximise the seating area then it's well worth thinking about building in seating, with possible storage underneath. Seating can be fixed to the walls so that the walls become the backs to the seat. Seating such as this works especially well when built in to the corner of a small space, therefore making an L-shaped bench. Brick or concrete block walling uprights with a timber slatted seat is usually more comfortable to sit on than stone or tiles. Cushions can be carried out from the house or possibly stored under the seat itself if there is enough room. Planters can be constructed of the same materials and at the same height of the built-in seat, which will create an opportunity to raise the level of the planting while harmonising the composition. Be careful when building against the outside wall of a house as the works may affect the damp-proof course.

Walls and boundaries

It is likely that the walls in areas such as these will dominate the feel of the whole space. As the garden will be small it is usually the walls and the other verticals that will have most impact and be seen regularly, so it is important to approach them first. Old brick walls, which are often dirty from the city pollution, tend to absorb light and add to the gloomy feel of the

Above: **Side alleys are often spaces to be viewed rather than used. Continuing the surface from the main area of the garden gives a cohesive look to the whole garden.**

space. These walls can easily be cleaned with a pressure washer, but will quickly get dirty again. Ideally, these walls should be exploited to help reflect light into the whole space. Brick walls can be cleaned and then painted a light colour. The effect of painting existing brick walls a light colour will accentuate each individual brick in a wall. For a more contemporary look to a garden, make the walling as smooth as possible. This can be achieved through rendering the walls before painting. Rendering will also make the painting and subsequent re-painting easier.

Uneven and shabby brick walls can also be effectively clad with various materials such as timber, bamboo screening or sheet metals. Marine plywood screwed into the wall can quickly create a flat surface, whereas fencing panels or timber slats can easily be screwed on to a simple frame to create interesting and original textures. The timber can then be stained or painted a light colour. Wood stains are now available in light colours and can be mixed together to produce some interesting shades.

Other materials, which can be used to lighten up the walls and boundaries of an area such as a basement well, are sheet metals. Copper, zinc or stainless steel sheets can easily be fixed to a wall and instantly change the feel of a small space as well as cover a multitude of sins. If left to weather, copper will attain a warm verdigris finish. It can also be polished or wiped with wire wool for varying finishes. Stainless steel and zinc will help by reflecting light into the adjoining room.

Split bamboo and light willow screening can be bought on a roll and used to clad a wall and add an interesting texture. The bamboo will only last a few years in comparison to the willow, but it is reflected in the price difference.

Trellis can be effectively used for fixing those climbing plants that aren't self-clinging. If the walls are to be painted, a good technique is to paint the trellis the same colour as the wall it is to be fixed to. This will create a much more subtle contrast of tone and texture between the two and will not detract from the effect of painting the walls a light colour. If you paint the walls a light colour

Opposite: **A shady area is not always a disadvantage when growing plants. There are many plants, such as hostas, fatsias and ferns, which will thrive in shade, and give a cool lush look to the garden.**

Above: **In a small space a well-placed mirror can increase the depth and mystery whilst at the same time bouncing light into the whole of the garden. Here it is used to break the harsh line of the corner in a wall.**

and fix a dark coloured trellis on to it this will often defeat the object as the overall effect will appear darker than the base colour of the wall.

Mirrors

The use of mirrors can, if executed well, work brilliantly in an awkward space, and increase the feeling of scope and mystery in a small garden. The size, shape and placing of the mirror are all important to create the effect you are looking for. It is generally advisable to be bold, and use large mirrors, which may seem out of proportion to the space itself, but will at least draw the eye and create the desired effect. The mirror itself becomes a canvas on which to paint a picture.

A whole wall with a mirror fixed on to it can visually double the size of the space as it will reflect not only all the other walls, but all the other items placed in the area. Furthermore, if a mirror covers the edges of a wall, it will mean you can't see the edges of the mirror and therefore you aren't quite sure where it ends. Planting climbers to hide the edges of the mirror will help to enhance the illusion.

A poorly placed mirror can make a garden look tacky. The angle of the mirror will affect what you see in it. If, for example, the first thing you see reflected is yourself, any creative illusion is completely shattered. Use timber battens behind one edge to change the angle of the mirror. Keep standing back to check exactly what is going to be reflected in the mirror. You need to be creative when devising your mirror-picture, and think about what you want to see. You might well prefer the reflection of a particular feature, a specimen architectural plant or a beautiful pot, than the reflection of a dull wall or messy planting, which will detract from the composition. You also need, of course, to think about the position from which you will mostly be seeing whatever it is you decide on.

Mirrored perspex is a safe alternative to a mirror and shouldn't need regular cleaning. If using a glass mirror it's important to frame it with a watertight frame, although a weathered mirror has the possible advantage of creating a specific antique look. The frame will also make it easier to fix to the wall without the need to drill holes in the mirror.

Pots and planting

When planting a backyard, alley or basement well, shade is likely to be the main issue to consider. High walls or fences can often dominate an area like this so a choice of shade tolerant climbers is critical. In cases where the plants will be viewed all year round it is, of course, important to think about how the plants will look in winter.

Evergreen climbers are limited, but there are some that have the necessary qualities to help the design along. Ivy is often perceived as a

Below: **Bold colours can help to add a contemporary look to a small garden. The smooth painted wall is the perfect backdrop for the black bamboo (*Phyllostachys nigra*), and the slate chipping mulch introduces a different texture whilst helping to retain moisture in the container.**

rather boring and common plant, but some of the varieties are perfect for these situations. The variegated ivies such as *Hedera* 'Gloire de Marengo' or 'Glacier' both have a crisp white margin to the leaf and will help brighten up a dark wall.

'In cases where the plants will be viewed all year round it is, of course, important to think about how the plants will look in winter'

The evergreen climber *Trachelospermum jasminoides* is an ideal plant for shady walls. It is generally thought of as being a sun lover, but it can thrive and flower well in the shade although it will not tolerate temperatures below 7°C. The small glossy dark green leaves clothe the stems right to the ground and the small white flowers have a strong, heady, jasmine scent in the summer.

Fatshedera lizei is a cross between a fatsia and an ivy. It is a sturdy evergreen plant, which can be trained up a wall without encroaching into the space too much. Its exotic-looking and deeply lobed, dark glossy leaves reflect the light well and therefore make it perfect for a shady wall.

Some people are not particularly fond of variegated plants, but they are incredibly useful when trying to brighten up a shady area. White, silver or gold margins to the leaves of a variegated plant, such as a variegated hosta or variegated fatsia, will really help to lift the composition and visually draw the plants out from the shade. The variegation also helps to contrast well with other plants and therefore gives more scope to the planting.

In a small space, the selection of plants has to be carefully considered. Each plant must have certain qualities, which can enhance and hold the small space around it. Sculptural shade-loving plants, such as fatsias, tree

Opposite: **This modern city house needs an equally bold garden to go with it. The circular raised bed and simple planting combine well with the colours and curves to complete the composition.**

ferns and some bamboos, are architectural and command their own space all year round without relying on their flowers for interest.

The pots in which the plants are grown are also important to the overall look of the space. Again, look for light or bright colours to help lift the space and manipulate the light. There are some fantastic glossy glazed pots, which come in whites and off-whites. The various greens of the plants will always look good planted in light coloured containers. Terracotta pots can easily be brightened up with a wash of paint.

In a small space, such as a basement well, it can look very effective if the pot or pots used seem slightly too large for the space. It will look much better than if they seem disproportionately small. The placing of pots in a small space is important for a contemporary feel. Don't be afraid to place pots and plants in regimented rows against a wall. It's obvious that the composition is not a natural occurrence so why attempt to overly soften it or make it look like it just happened that way? Be bold and assured when buying plants and pots as the resulting composition will speak for itself.

Often pots that get placed in gardens like these aren't easily visible as they are placed on the ground. The planting can end up at too low a level. A good technique is to install some shelving against the walls and put the smaller pots on to these shelves. This will break up the wall and raise the plants nearer to eye level where they can be viewed and appreciated.

Lighting

As these areas are regularly viewed all year round the addition of lighting can help to make a complete composition and enlarge the feeling of space from within the property. The flooding of light from above to create a wash of light on the whole area is really effective. If carried out successfully it can give the impression that the glass in the window or doors has completely disappeared and the outside space is integrated with the interior. In the summer, the lighting will help turn the garden into a

genuine outdoor room. In the winter months, the flick of a switch can bring the garden space alive to be appreciated as a composition from inside.

Maintenance

The maintenance of these types of spaces is relatively easy as the space is usually small. In brief, any plants grown in pots will have to be re-potted at some stage. Shrubs will need new pots roughly every three years whereas perennials can be lifted and divided and then repotted in the same container. With shrubs this is the time to consider whether it's the pot you need to replace or the plant itself. If the plant is getting too large for the space then it's often easier and cheaper to replace the plant with a smaller one of the same variety or another appropriate plant to change or freshen up the composition.

With shady areas there is usually the problem of slimy residue build-up on the surfaces, whether stone, brick or deck, although a rougher surface will be less slippery even with this residue. Pressure washers are easy to buy or hire and are ideal for cleaning up these surfaces as necessary – usually once or twice a year. They will clean up the surface almost back to new without the unnecessary use of any bleach or weedkillers. Make sure that the area has good drainage and that the rainwater drains are clear before starting on the rather rewarding task.

As a last word on this subject be careful about rubbish. The side alleys along a house can act as a vortex for the wind. If you aren't too careful, the whole neighbourhood's rubbish can quickly end up in your garden. A strategically placed barrier, whether it's a gate or trellis with a finer mesh attached, will help to keep this rubbish out.

Left: **With a small backyard think how you want the space to be used. Here a built-in bench plus the table and chairs provide enough seating for a** small party. The planting of the golden bamboos, date palm (*Phoenix canariensis*) and banana add height without too much spread.

the minimalist garden

When successfully executed, the minimalist approach can be tranquil, refreshing, exciting and sublime all at the same time. Originally an eastern concept, largely based on the philosophies of Zen Buddhism, minimalist spaces are primarily designed for contemplation and the clearing of the mind. This particular style of garden is possibly more relevant in the West today than it has ever been. It can be perfectly suited for the making of an outdoor room in a hectic modern city, where it is hard to find a place that is truly calm and peaceful away from the stresses of urban life. The minimalist garden, although it is not a modern concept, can be the perfect antidote to the busy modern lifestyle.

What's more, the fundamentals of minimalism are well suited to small city gardens. The minimalist garden can successfully link the outdoor space to the interior, leave the garden space open and flexible for a variety of uses, incorporate modern materials and genuinely create a low-maintenance garden.

Absolutely any garden can be approached in the minimalist style. All the types of garden discussed in this book can be designed along minimalist principles. Indeed, minimalism is in essence a set of aesthetic principles, which can be imposed on to any of these types of gardens without them becoming too thematic, as they might with, say, a Japanese or Moroccan garden. Thematic gardens rely heavily on instant effect and the appeal can quickly wear thin and seem out of date. The minimalist garden is very much about control over the whole space from concept through to implementation and there is usually a strong sense of formality in the organisation and manipulation of the space. Rather than trying to shy away from its origins of being designed by attempting to copy nature, it's a type of garden that revels in its unambiguous position of obviously being created by man.

Above: Rather than attempting to recreate nature, the city garden revels in its unambiguous position of obviously being created by man. The varying forms of the lavender stoechas and the white agapanthus are seen clearly against a strong background colour.

Previous pages: **The simplicity of minimalism when well executed can create exciting compositions in the city garden. Here the rhythm of the box balls is set off perfectly by the uncluttered smooth plastered wall.**

Another advantage of this style is that these days the garden is expected to look good pretty much all year round. This perennial beauty is something the minimalist garden can realistically achieve. It is most often designed to be a permanent composition. There may be seasonal changes within the planting, but it is more likely that this will be viewed in the more fleeting form of, say, a single tree looking stunning in its autumn colour. This is a quality that will take the composition to a higher level without detracting from the all-year-round composition.

The minimal style of garden is an acquired taste and may not be what everyone is looking for. Critics of this style of gardening may see these compositions as stark or over simplified, but the whole philosophy, which can be summed up by the simple phrase 'Less is More', can no doubt lead to the creation of some fantastically imaginative spaces.

The limiting of the garden elements is all part of creating a Zen garden. The detailed placing of rocks, water and plants to create the all-important interaction is crucial to the overall composition of an Oriental garden. Remove or misplace any one of these elements and the garden will feel incomplete; add just one too many elements and it will feel cluttered and unbalanced. The principle of restraint is of utmost importance to a garden of this style.

In the West, minimalism is often connected with modernism, being the process of paring down the design to the absolute essentials of form and function. This approach casts off the fussy detailing, which has been so highly regarded in the past. Clean lines and simple compositions are part of both the modern and minimalist look. We are all becoming more design conscious and have high expectations regarding well-designed products,

Below: **Angular and highly architectural layouts work well when designing minimalist gardens. The shadows on the walls and steps define the structure, and the still reflective pond will subtly change the otherwise permanent composition.**

whether it's a kitchen tap or a motor car. Good design is the art of combining the efficient and ease-of-use of a product with its all-important desirable looks. Modern design is changing rapidly and modern materials are being embraced by all groups of design-led industries: architects, interior designers, industrial designers and product designers. In the past, the garden – as far as design and products are concerned – has been a bit of an afterthought in comparison to these industries, but more recently has become closely connected with all these other aspects of design.

Natural landscapes, such as limestone rock formations, coastal sand-scapes and naturalised woodland areas, are just a few examples of how nature works and can produce a beautiful minimal composition. These landscapes may include plants that have been limited through a natural selection process. The minimal garden is not attempting to recreate nature in one's own space. Inspiration can be taken from nature, but minimalism will rarely attempt to imitate it. Rather, it is a highly artificial form of aesthetic, which has been manipulated sometimes to an extreme.

After having read this chapter about minimalist gardens you may find that you've been inspired to rid yourself of the clutter in your life or you may feel that this type of garden just wouldn't be right for you, for a variety of reasons. The discipline and limitations you need to impose call for a certain way of thinking and way of living. It is unlikely that you can achieve a purely minimal garden if you know that you are not self-disciplined. It is important for a garden to reflect your own personality and there is no doubt that to approach a garden in this way, it is important to be comfortable with the concept. It will mean being ruthless with the existing site, and getting rid of anything that does not fit in with the overall plan or it simply won't in the end work well. The rewards, however, are to be gained for those who dare to be bold and uncompromising.

If you don't want to go the whole way, there are certain elements in a minimal approach to design that are well worth considering as they can help

Opposite: **The strong architecture of the building throws a perfect shadow on the wall to complete the composition. The gap in the wall frames a view to draw the eye through and beyond.**

Previous pages: **The chunky timber raised bed with tall *Phormium tenax* contrasts well with the sleek interior and provides privacy from overlooking apartments.**

Below: **The seamless transition between inside and out is achieved by running the paving through the two spaces. The large glass windows bring light into the property whilst making the garden somewhere to be viewed all year.**

achieve a contemporary look in any other style of garden. A well-executed and designed look hinges on some basic elements, all of which can be seen in the minimalist garden, but can also be applied elsewhere.

Linking the exterior to the interior

The connecting of the outside space to the interior is an important consideration when designing a minimalist garden. It is important that the garden feels directly linked to the interior of your house to create a cohesive living space. The balance and seamless transition between the interior and exterior spaces, which is so often sought after when trying to

create an outdoor room, is highly achievable through minimalism. The blurring between the two spaces can be achieved simply by installing large windows or glass doors and walls, which are increasingly being incorporated into many city houses and apartments to maximise natural light. Elements such as flooring materials, wall colours and detailing from the interior can successfully be taken into the garden and vice versa to harmonise the space. For example, if the main room leading to the garden has a slate tiled floor the continuation of this flooring into the garden will strongly connect the spaces and help to link the two together.

Strong geometry, such as square or rectangular grids and formula proportions, which are usually found in the interior of any building, can be echoed if not identically replicated in the garden to achieve the link. The strong lines of buildings, such as where the doors and windows are placed, can become a good starting point when designing the layout of the garden. The extension of these lines if laid flat on to the plan of the garden can help to make sense of the garden space, giving it good proportions as well as keeping the close link between the two.

Above: **Minimalist design can create a flexible space with a variety of uses. This roof garden is also left uncluttered to maximize the extended view.**

'The connecting of the outside space to the interior is an important consideration when designing a minimalist garden'

Flexibility

The minimalist style can create the most flexible of gardens as far as the variety of its uses goes. A minimalist garden will usually attempt to maximise the space into a single composition and is therefore unlikely to divide the garden into a series of rooms or smaller spaces as might be the case with the way other gardens have been treated. There has been a trend of creating a series of rooms, which can provide privacy, mystery and drama in a garden. This technique can work well in larger gardens but can also limit the flexibility that the whole space can be used for.

In a minimalist garden, the ratio of hard landscaping materials, such as paving or pathways, to plants is usually greater than in a more conventional or traditional garden. This can lead to the whole of the garden being much more functional and available for a wide variety of uses. For example, if the main area of a garden is predominantly paved and left clear then the space can be used for pretty much anything, just like an uncluttered room within the house.

The minimalist style can work well as a family garden where the demands on the space range from entertaining through to children's ball games. If the garden is to be used as a play area for children it is likely there will be fewer plants to get damaged. As the aim of a minimalist garden is to create a tranquil place it makes the perfect setting for reading or quiet contemplation. With the increase in people working from home, a garden like this can easily be somewhere to focus on work successfully.

Layout

A strong bold concept is essential when embarking on a garden of this nature. The design of the garden layout should be developed from the basic functions and needs of the space and the garden owner's interaction with it. The process of paring down to the absolute essentials can lead to some exciting designs, which capture the essence of the space.

A design may initially develop from no more than a couple of decisions, such as the need to increase privacy from an overlooking office block or the desire to sit in the area of the garden that will catch the evening sun. The decision of how exactly you will screen that office block – will you use a solid fence, trellis, hedge or a single standing tree? – are vital design

decisions that will determine the look of the whole space. What about the seating area? Is it a single timber bench sitting on beach pebbles or a painted set of chairs and table on a generous slate-tiled terrace? It is important to be able to visualise the interaction and relationship between these two elements, as they will affect the overall mood of the garden.

The strong use of geometric shapes is found in most successful city gardens and the often highly geometric layout of the minimalist garden can sometimes be as easily read from within the garden as if looking at a plan from above. The strong lines created through this geometry of the hard landscaping are often accentuated and emphasised rather than any attempt being made to blur or soften them with planting. For example, if a retaining wall has been designed to make a strong statement by boldly cutting through a garden then the top edge of the wall makes more sense if it is left clear.

Minimalism doesn't rely on decorative techniques. It is the manipulation of the space itself that leads to the success of the design. The overall architectural nature of a garden in this style is often shown through the clarity of certain construction techniques. Building techniques that show the essence of the whole structure are often accentuated and revel in their simplicity, even though they may actually be rather complex.

Clean lines within a bold simple layout are important to achieve the minimal look. The detailing in a minimalist garden is more likely to take the form of simple repetitive themes rather than an ornate or fussy format. For example, an area of paving may change the unit size of the same material or lay a line of a smaller unit to delineate almost sub-consciously certain areas within a garden. Rhythm, often created through repetition of plants

Left: **The garden design should be developed around the basic functions and needs of the space. Clean lines with a bold simple layout are an important factor in achieving the** **minimal look. This indoor/outdoor courtyard is closely linked to the architecture of the building itself and is far removed from the traditional concept of the garden.**

or materials, is crucial to soothe the eye. Subtle contrasts of light and tone, rather than the clashing contrasts of shapes and vibrant colours, are employed to create the all-important tranquil mood of the garden.

Landscaping materials

As described, the hard-landscaping materials are often higher up the agenda in a minimalist garden than in other more conventional and softer forms of garden design and are absolutely crucial to the success of the minimalist look. In a large space, a minimal garden can be successful while being soft and incorporating lawns and large areas of planting. In a small city garden, however, a lawn is often impractical as it needs plenty of maintenance and cannot cope with heavy traffic. It will also reduce the hours a garden can be used as it takes a long time to dry out once wet.

The importance put on to the hard landscaping helps a garden of this style to sit comfortably in an urban setting and it is not inconceivable that a garden can be created without a single plant, as are some of the Zen gravel gardens in Japan. The city itself is all about imposing ourselves on to the landscape to create a setting far detached from the rural world and the garden is all about our need to organise nature. The minimalist garden offers the opportunity to manipulate the space as desired and take the concept within the garden to the extreme.

The discipline and restraint necessary to create a minimalist garden must be carried throughout the hard landscaping aspects of the work. This is crucial to achieving the particular feel of such a garden. It is important to play around with different samples of materials to help to visualise what the whole garden will look like. There isn't a particular winning formula and the choice today is greater than it has ever been. However, natural materials will always look great in any style of garden: timber, stone, granite and slate for example. These materials would probably be most people's first choice if their budget can cover it, for they are expensive.

Opposite: **Concrete is a highly versatile material that is starting to shed its rather poor reputation. The spiky accents of the *Agave americana* and purple phormiums contrast well with the smooth planes of the coloured concrete.**

Above: **Using pots or planters the same colour as the wall behind will create a more subtle contrast in form and tone than picking a strong contrasting colour. The large expanse of light pebbles harmonises the space, whilst introducing a different texture.**

Synthetic materials, such as concrete, glass and steel, can be good value for money as well as giving a contemporary look and working well in the composition of a minimalist garden. Concrete is a fabulous material and it is starting to shed its rather poor reputation. It can be formed into any shape and be finished in a wide range of textures and colours. One of its chief advantages is that it appears seamless, without any joints, and therefore can be used to create large flat planes either as a paving material or for walling, ponds or seating. It is a material that is far too effective, affordable and flexible for a wide range of projects to overlook.

When choosing materials for a garden like this, as a general rule the unit size of the material used should be proportionate to the overall size of the garden. For example, in a small garden use a small unit size such as a slate tile, granite sett or brick for paving. Use larger units such as stone slabs or gravels (which will visually read as a whole unit rather than thousands of small pebbles) for larger areas in larger gardens. Random mixtures and combinations of differing materials can often look messy or fussy and detract from the overall composition.

As with all gardens, however, the important factor is how the materials are put together and the relationship between each other. This is the thing that will make the composition successful.

Boundaries

The boundaries in a minimalist garden are often treated in the opposite way to other, more conventional gardens, where the walls or fences are usually disguised through planting in an attempt to lose them. In more conventional cases, by visually losing the boundaries, the garden sometimes appears larger. The mind is tricked by the eye as to where the actual physical limits of the garden lie. In the minimalist garden, however, the endeavour is generally to keep the focus within the garden. This internalises the space and connects the garden to the house rather than to the landscape beyond. This is achieved by making sure the boundaries are unified in some way, easily visible and left uncluttered. Walls can be clad with screening or painted where there is a muddled variety of existing finishes. It may be possible to plant climbers on the walls. Remember though, that as the boundaries are at eye-level when standing, they are likely to be the first thing you notice – so they need to be dealt with in the same uncluttered and restrained way as the rest of the garden.

Planting

Once the layout and landscaping work has been undertaken, consider the planting. Approach the selection of plants in this type of garden in the same sympathetic, but rather ruthless way. Plants all have their own particular distinguishing qualities, which must be used sympathetically within the design. Foliage, outline shape, height, movement, colour, scent and flower are all qualities that a single plant may possess. It's these qualities that need to be carefully considered and edited in a minimalist garden. There may be a plant that has the most heavenly scent in spring, but for the rest of the year lacks any strong form and looks messy. Or an evergreen foliage plant, which looks great most of the year but has flowers which clash with all the other plants.

With the minimalist garden, it is important that the choice of the plants and the placing of them are carried out confidently and with precision. There are no hard and fast rules to planting a minimalist garden as far as choosing particular types of plants, as would be the case when trying to create a tropical or Mediterranean look. In these cases, the selection of plants is limited to those which

Below: **Successful planting in a minimalist garden is limited and ruthless. The shape of these box balls in galvanized steel containers makes a clean bold statement.**

would grow, or look as if they would grow, in a tropical or Mediterranean climate. In a minimalist garden, the decision of which plants will be appropriate is not made on this basis; it's more the interaction between the plants and the other garden materials that matters. The choice of colour of any flowers is equally important in a minimalist garden – see the section on colour (page 94).

'The space you leave between and around the plants is as important as the plants themselves'

The rhythm of the planting design determines and manipulates the way the eye reads the landscape. Repetition of the same plants, sometimes in large quantity, will help to harmonise a space much more successfully than a mixed composition of various colours and textures. Blocks of plants work well and are viewed like blocks of colours in a painting. This doesn't mean that each block should be a different and strongly contrasting colour, in fact they will look better if the contrasts are subtle. This is where it's important to remember that green is a colour that has great variety. The different shades of foliage, whether they are, say, grey-greens, golden-greens, acid-greens, black-greens or purple-greens, work fantastically well together.

The space you leave between and around the plants is as important as the plants themselves. I often find that with plants it is incredibly difficult to limit yourself – especially if you are a plant lover and collector. However, if you are unable to be disciplined about the planting, you will not be able to achieve a pure minimal look. In some circumstances the varieties used in a garden may be limited to as few as three or four. If that sounds extreme, perhaps the minimalist garden is not for you.

Opposite left: **Plants all have particular qualities that make them suitable for specific uses. The unashamed and regimented manipulation of the black grass** *Ophiopogon planiscapus* **'Nigrescens' brings a powerful mood to this courtyard.**

Opposite right: **The planting of a minimalist garden needs to be carried out confidently and with precision. The strict discipline of limiting plant varieties is important to achieve this look.**

Above: **Pure symmetry often helps to make sense of a small space. Proportion and the relationship between materials is the key to the success of this minimal garden.**

As the aim will probably be to create a reasonably permanent composition to be viewed all year round, from inside as well as out, the plants must be chosen accordingly. The architectural qualities of the plants, whether it's the huge arching and deeply cut fronds of a tree fern or the rounded form of a clipped box ball, are usually the most important characteristics. Do consider the solidity of these architectural plants. Substantial plants such as box, yew, phormiums and laurels all carry a certain weight, which help to tie the overall picture to the ground. The more wispy and flowing plants, like the bamboos and tall grasses, are more delicate and will blow gracefully in the wind, adding movement to the garden.

Pots and furniture

Although the minimalist garden doesn't rely on decoration for its success there are ways of adding certain elements to keep the composition fresh and interactive, but any addition must be placed sensitively and with regard to all the other elements in the garden. With a minimalist garden even a single misplaced pot can ruin the composition rather than enhancing it. With pots, pick one shape and type of finish rather than a mish-mash of different shapes, colours and sizes. Ideally, the pots chosen should be the simplest of shapes with very little detail or intricacy. If there are any strong colours, such as painted walls, then the colours of the pots are important in relation to this colour. A good technique is to paint planters the same colours as the walls they are placed in front of so the composition is focused more on the tonal differences created by the relief and shadows cast on to the walls. The finish of the pot should blend in with the composition rather than trying to fight for attention.

The same principles go for any furniture, which may be included into the design or brought into the garden when required. It is important that the choice of furniture material is understated, so avoid ornate or fussy designs and patterned fabrics.

Lighting

As the manipulation of light and tone are important factors in the minimalist approach it follows that lighting can be integrated to play an important role and genuinely add a fresh dimension and change the way a garden is seen. Fittings should be as simple and unobtrusive as possible, concentrating on the quality and type of light they give, rather than bringing attention to the actual fittings themselves. Lighting should ideally be subtle and understated. This can be achieved through the repetition of low-wattage fittings rather than the dramatic lighting from powerful uplighters. Hidden lighting laid in a linear formation, such as recessed fittings under step risers or seats, can help to keep the strong structure of a minimalist garden at night. Washes of lights on to flat planes of wall can also be very effective and reiterate the shape and geometry of the garden.

Colour

The introduction of colour has to be carefully considered in a minimalist garden and balanced overall with the consideration of all the above elements: plants, materials and lighting. The natural colours of stone and wood will rarely clash in a garden, especially when they have been weathered by the elements and it therefore makes these great favourites.

Another way to introduce colour into the minimalist garden is in the form of painting or staining. The painting of garden walls and house walls can bring the two together, linking the garden cohesively to the house. Minimalist gardens often implement light colours (white or off-white) for various reasons. Light colours will make the subtle textural and light contrasts of the space easy to read in relief: the walls of art galleries are almost always painted white so that the wall colours don't compete with the paintings hung on the wall. Plants are the equivalent of these works of art and demand the right backdrop too. Shadows cast on light walls can also bring an interesting and ever-changing aspect to the garden as the sun moves round the sky throughout the day.

Strong colours demand attention and can act as a distraction from the calm and soothing intention of the garden. The addition of bold colours, such as yellows, blues or reds, however, can also be amazingly powerful and act as the perfect foil for plants, but the choice of the colour, as with everything in the minimalist garden, is absolutely crucial. Fortunately, colour through painting can easily be introduced into the design towards the later stages and can be approached in an experimental way by trying different colours to see which work well. Small sample pots are easily available from paint stockists to play around with.

Colour introduced by the flowers of plants can really make or break a minimalist garden. The colour of flowers can add sublime, fleeting qualities, which take the composition to a higher plane. There are some stunning specimen plants, such as *Magnolia grandiflora* or wisteria, which, when in flower, can stop you in your tracks. Plants such as these, when incorporated into a garden composition, will add the beautiful colours only nature can produce. It is important to visualise how they will look for the rest of the year and whether they have more to offer than just the flower. A minimalist garden may be able to afford the luxury of a stunner or two, but be careful as every garden needs definition and structure rather than lots of little fireworks going off throughout the year.

Maintenance

Generally, the minimal look will lead to a very low-maintenance garden, which is so often a major consideration with someone who has little time to garden. Yet even with minimal gardens lack of adequate maintenance will quickly make a garden look untidy or messy and therefore be an uninviting space to enter – let alone relax in. However, as it is likely that the garden will contain mainly hard surfaces, this will make the areas easy to keep clean. As the plants are more likely to be sculptural or foliage plants, they won't need the regular attention (staking, deadheading and cutting back in the autumn) that most flowering perennials demand. The mulching of planting areas with materials such as gravels, cockleshells or bark on top of a landscape fabric will considerably reduce the need for watering and help to suppress any weeds.

Above: **A low-maintenance garden that will always look good. The solid, sculptural quality of the 'cloud pruned' box holds the interest, and fits the space perfectly.**

the conservatory garden

The conservatory epitomizes the change in the way that space is so highly valued in the city and reflects the increasing need for flexible living areas. In the past, the conservatory was viewed as being more of a greenhouse added on to a building, a place to grow exotic specimens as a pastime or to over-winter the less hardy varieties of plants. More recently though, developments in glass technology and insulation techniques combined with exciting designs and architecture have led to the conservatory casting off its staid and traditional image.

These days 'conservatory' is a loose term and can be used for anything from a kitchen, playroom, study, office or library to artist's studio or dining room, or a combination of all of these thrown into one. It can be set at ground floor level or the building may have opportunities to site one at a higher level, on the first or the second floor where fantastic panoramic views across the city can be seen. The conservatory can be the ideal multifunctional space. It is usable all year round and can even change its function

Previous pages: **Developments in glass technology have increased innovation in design – shown here in this lean-to style conservatory.**

Below: **Conservatories can make the perfect transition between house and garden. Glass panels increase the feeling of space.**

with the season. Maybe it can be used as a dining room in the summer and a spare bedroom throughout the winter?

Natural light is one of the most valued commodities in the city. Wherever possible, light should be exploited and manipulated to help to increase the feeling of space, and therefore decrease the feeling of claustrophobia that an urban environment can instil. Modern urban houses will more often than not try to maximise the use of glass whereas

older properties are constantly being renovated and refurbished with more modern materials to suit a change in city living.

A conservatory can also help to increase the amount of light directly coming into the main areas of a property. Once a conservatory has been installed it will instantly create a physical barrier against the elements. This, in turn, will lead to the possibility of removing internal walls in part or entirely and therefore let the light flood into the rest of the house. Side alleys between houses, which are often awkward and dead spaces, can be glassed over and incorporated into the main rooms of the house to make them bigger.

The conservatory can also make the perfect transition between house and garden. It becomes a space that links both the garden directly to the house, and the house to the garden and at the same time has a unique quality unlike any other room in the house. Of course, the conservatory can also be the place for its more traditional function – to house exciting and varied plants. A completely different micro-climate to that of the garden outside will inspire its owners to grow plants without the fear of frosts or harsh winds. These plants will help to create a garden like no other: an exotic garden with scented and colourful plants, which can be the perfect all-year-round retreat from a busy city life.

Conservatory design

It is unlikely that a conservatory would have been built at the same time as the house, so it will therefore be an addition to the property. I don't see the point in building something new to look old, so if you are building a conservatory the main consideration is how to make a contemporary structure complement the existing building and look just right or possibly even stunning. Glass is a fantastic medium and the more glass there is in a conservatory, the better. As it is translucent it will rarely clash with anything and the technology to build strong frameless conservatories is here and quickly developing. If you choose to have a custom-built conservatory you will need to consult both an architect and an engineer as even a simple structure needs planning consent as well as complex calculations. Then there are all the structural implications as well as considerations such as how much heat will be lost if an internal wall is knocked through.

A conservatory has to be designed sensitively as it will not only be viewed in its relation to the house and garden from the outside, but how the garden will look when viewed through the conservatory from the inside. Too many small frames will break up the composition from inside and look too fussy from outside. If individual panels are to be used to make the conservatory, try to install them so they are as large as possible without losing too much of the building's proportion, maybe double the size of other windows in the house. Ideally, the doors and windows should also be generous so that in the summer the conservatory can be opened up to help keep it cool and to keep it closely linked with the garden.

If the conservatory has a frame, carefully consider what colour you want the frame to be. White is the most commonly used colour, but tends to be too strong visually and sits awkwardly with the more natural colours of plants. Natural wood frames, or a more subdued painted colour such as a dark green or grey, will blend in better with the garden. Metallic frames will give a strong contemporary feel, and can be picked up elsewhere in the garden with metallic pots, or silver-leaved plants.

The whole of the conservatory should be as generous as possible. It is amazing how the space will shrink when a table, chairs and a few pots and plants are brought in. Remember, though, that the space will more than likely be taken directly from the garden. If you have a tiny garden, make sure that the space left is still of some value, or you may look back and wish you had made the conservatory bigger or not built one in the first place.

Right: **The blue frames and blue pots intensify the green of the plants, and create a cohesive look to the space. Modern interior furniture helps to connect the conservatory closely to the inside living areas.**

Surface materials are important, too, as they have to be practical and help make the link between the house and garden. Try to connect the conservatory with either the internal floor or the paving in the garden rather than introducing a completely new material, as it will create a visual barrier rather than easing the link. The ultimate in smooth transition is to have a surface laid from the inside of the house, through the conservatory and into the garden as a terrace. The material would need to be tough, such as a limestone or granite, as it would have to be able to withstand the elements thrown at it outside. Be careful not to use overly smooth surfaces such polished limestone tiles outside as when the area gets wet it will become slippery and dangerous. If a timber floor is used inside and echoed outside with a deck, remember that the deck will undoubtedly weather more quickly than the internal floor, and change the look considerably. Drainage is a consideration when building a conservatory. If a stone floor is to be laid, it is worth trying to incorporate a central drain or a channel grating along one of the sides of the conservatory. This will make cleaning the conservatory easier as it can be hosed down with water. There is also the excess water from the watering of plants, as well as the inevitable odd leak and spillage.

Siting

The siting of a new conservatory is more important than you may think. It is a temptation to construct it in the sunniest spot, such as a south-facing wall, but beware: the problem with conservatories is that they can become unbearably hot – even with pull-down shades. It is impossible to relax properly in a place when the heat is

Below: **A perfect spot to take time out. The conservatory is also essential to overwinter less hardy container-grown plants, which can be taken into the garden for more impact during summer months.**

overbearing. However, there may not be too many options as to where to site the conservatory, indeed, there may be only one place for it.

If the site isn't shaded by trees or another property an east-facing wall will catch the morning sun; a west-facing wall will catch the late afternoon/evening sun, and a north wall is unlikely to have any direct sun at all. Large windows, which can be easily opened, will help to control the temperature and allow air to circulate freely.

Pots, planters or growing in the ground?

When planning a conservatory consider leaving planting spaces so that plants can be grown straight in the ground. Although all plants can do well in pots, the more room there is for their roots to grow, the better. The rate of growth in a conservatory is greater than in the garden as plants will be growing pretty much all year round. They will quickly outgrow their pots, and will need regular re-potting. If the foundation layout of the conservatory allows, consider incorporating some planting spaces into the scheme before the flooring goes down. Large troughs can also be sunk into the ground to increase the depth of planting.

As with any garden, when growing plants in pots the important thing is to find a type of pot or planter that fits in with the style of the surrounding area. To create a designed, contemporary look stick to the same style of pots throughout the conservatory and, ideally, carry the same pots through into the garden as well. The echoing of any pots and style of planting into the garden or vice versa will only help to link the two spaces together.

Irrigation

Regular watering is vital in a conservatory for a variety of reasons. All the plants will probably be grown in containers of some variety or other and these containers will quickly dry out without regular watering. As the

Above: **Adjustable shades help to regulate the heat of a conservatory. This chunky wooden planter fits well into the style of this contemporary design.**

conservatory will be closed to the elements there will be no rainwater to irrigate the plants naturally, so all the watering will need to be done artificially. Watering by hand with a hose or watering can is time-consuming and easily forgotten. In the heat of the summer most plants will dry out quickly. Even a long weekend without water can cause some of the more moisture-loving plants to suffer.

'The most common mistake is attempting to grow plants that require a minimum temperature that cannot be maintained at night'

To ensure that your plants are getting watered regularly, whether there is someone there or not, it is best to install a computerised watering system. Try to get a tap installed inside the conservatory so the system can be connected up to it without having to feed a pipe through a window from outside. The nozzle-drip irrigation systems are the best for pots as they will water each pot individually, won't splash all over the floor and can be regulated for the needs of each plant. If the conservatory doesn't have a free-draining floor surface it is important to make sure that each pot or trough has a tray to catch the excess water. A tray will also reduce the amount of watering necessary.

Light and temperature

The amount of light a conservatory will get is dependent on its siting. It will also be a major factor in the choice of plants. A shadier conservatory will have a relatively even temperature, and is the ideal place to grow the more luscious foliage plants. A sunny conservatory will have a greater range between night and day temperatures, and will

Opposite: **The siting of the conservatory is important. On a south-facing aspect make sure there's enough shading from the sun. A grapevine will help to create shade, and still reflect the change in the seasons.**

probably need shading to help keep the temperatures down in the summer. The high light levels of a sunny conservatory lead to the right conditions for the more showy flowering plants to be grown.

The most common mistake is attempting to grow plants that require a minimum temperature that cannot be maintained at night time. In most cases, the conservatory is heated by an extension of the domestic central heating system. At night, when the heating system goes off, the temperature in the conservatory will drop considerably. Find out the minimum temperature that can be easily maintained, and plant accordingly rather than trying to grow plants in too cold an environment.

Planting

The conservatory creates a fantastic opportunity to grow a far wider variety of plants than could normally be grown in an outdoor garden, as the temperatures are unlikely to get really cold and frosts will be kept out by the glass roof. There are some plants that will live permanently in the conservatory, but there are also plenty of plants that can be taken outdoors on to the terrace in the summer and brought back into the shelter of the conservatory for the winter. These plants actually like to be aired throughout the summer. They will help to decorate, and add an exotic flavour to, the terrace.

When planting a conservatory for a contemporary look it is best to stick to the same design principles of planting a garden. Look for combinations of height and leaf texture. In a conservatory it is probably even more

tempting to grow one of everything than would be the case in a garden. But if you can discipline yourself to larger quantities of fewer varieties it will come across as a more designed space. A single stunning specimen, such as a palm or tree fern, can sometimes be enough planting in a small conservatory.

Palms

Palms are naturally architectural in shape and will instantly help to introduce height into a conservatory. There are plenty of palms, such as the beautiful Mexican blue palm (*Brahea armata*) with its silver-blue fan-shaped leaves, which can stay in the conservatory or be put out on to the terrace for the summer. It will tolerate temperatures of -10°C when mature so if it gets too big for the conservatory it can become a permanent fixture in the garden. The widely available kentia palm (*Howea forsteriana*) is perfect for the shady conservatory. It is a tall, arching palm, which needs little looking after and looks great when planted in groups or in a symmetrical scheme. The pygmy date palm (*Phoenix roebelenii*) will develop a slim trunk after a few years, and its weeping fronds give it a graceful delicate habit.

Left: **Even a small conservatory earns its space in the city. Planting it fully will have the effect of drawing the space inwards and making it even more intimate.**

Right: **The grey tiles used as a flooring surface and continued on the walls give a contemporary feel to this conservatory. It also makes the maintenance easy with a regular hose-down.**

Bananas

The bananas have huge fresh green leaves, which will add a tropical flavour to any conservatory. *Musa acuminata* 'Dwarf Cavendish' has yellow flower spikes in summer on a red or purple stem. Small yellow edible bananas follow. *Musa basjoo* is a hardy banana, which will thrive in a conservatory but can be taken into the garden when it gets too big. The bananas will do well in sun or shade if well fed and watered, but are more likely to fruit with plenty of sun.

Flowering plants

The bird of paradise (*Strelitzia reginae*) has large, graceful, bluey-green leaves, which are the perfect foil to the most stunning, exotic, bird-shaped flowers. They will take a few years to flower at first, but will flower reliably once established. They need plenty of sun.

Plumbago auriculata is an easy and reliable climbing plant for the conservatory. It has clusters of soft blue flowers, which last for weeks in summer. It will need to be trained up a trellis or have wires fixed to a wall. The striking, trumpet-shaped and fragrant flowers of the daturas and brugmansias make them a great plant for the conservatory. They can be moved into the garden for the summer, and often flower well into the autumn.

Citrus trees

The shiny, evergreen leaves, dream-scented flowers and colourful edible fruits, make citrus trees – oranges, lemons, grapefruits, mandarins, kumquats and calamondins – probably the best individual plants for the conservatory. They all need plenty of light and as constant a temperature as possible. Regular feeding and watering will produce plenty of flowers. *Citrus x meyeri* 'Meyer' is one of the easiest lemons, which flowers and fruits

Opposite: **An extra room to the house. Asplenium ferns, cycad palm and strelitzia will all thrive in the frost-free microclimate a conservatory creates.**

almost continuously. x *Citrofortunella microcarpa* – the calamondin orange – does particularly well in pots and produces miniature oranges all year round. It likes to be aired in the garden during the summer.

Ferns

In a shady conservatory, the ferns come into their own as they do in a shady garden. They really help to create a lush look to the planting. The less hardy tree ferns such as *Dicksonia squarrosa* and *Cyathea dealbata* are beautiful, ancient plants with their coarse trunks and long fresh fronds. They thrive in the shaded conservatory as long as they are watered regularly. As their roots are on the trunk itself rather than at the base of the plant, try to get an irrigation drip feed to the top of the trunk, so that the stem is constantly damp.

There are other conservatory ferns such as *Asplenium bulbiferum* (mother fern), which has large glossy mid-green leaves 60-90cm (2-3ft) across. *Nephrolepsis exaltata* (Boston fern) has arching finely cut fronds, and is the perfect conservatory fern for a hanging basket.

Maintenance

The maintenance of a conservatory is more likely to consist of cleaning windows than any of the more conventional gardening chores. Hopefully, this task will have been considered during the design stage, as it will need to be done fairly regularly. Tall conservatories will need a squeegee with a long handle or a tall set of step ladders. Again, a hard-wearing flooring such as stone will be the most practical for any drips or spillages.

Most conservatory plants like regular misting with soft water. It will keep the humidity levels up and stop leaves from turning brown. A common problem with indoor plants is to over water. Except with moisture-loving plants, such as bananas and ferns, give each plant plenty of water and let the top of the soil dry out before watering again. I always find that indoor plants don't like to be pampered – a little neglect seems to work wonders!

Left: Natural light is a sought-after commodity in a city environment. An atrium-style conservatory increases the natural light into otherwise dark areas. As it is too small to be used as a living space it becomes the place to create a permanent composition.

the water garden

Water brings a garden to life. In fact, water is life itself. Without it nothing living would survive. The movement and sound of water can add a whole new dimension to the city garden, which other features and installations simply can't compete with. In the heat of the summer, water will bring a cool and serene presence to the outdoor room and help you to fully unwind from urban life. With the modern city being so detached from the natural world, water can also reconnect the city dweller to the basic and essential forms of nature, and magically catch the imagination. Moving water will draw the attention of both adults and children and add a sense of play to a garden.

When planning water into a design, be careful with the composition. Water is often associated with more natural-looking gardens and is designed to give the impression that it has naturally occurred. In an urban setting the suggestion that the water feature happens to be a part of the natural landscape seems simply too far fetched. This is one of the reasons that it is

Previous pages: **With reliable modern materials water can be successfully contained and manipulated in almost any form. The city water garden encourages the use of modern materials rather than attempting to imitate natural forms.**

important to incorporate the water deliberately and boldly into a city garden. Water has so many thought-provoking qualities that it is not necessary to disguise its reason for being in an urban situation.

Formal shapes, such as rectangular, circular or square water features, sit more comfortably in the outdoor room and also fit well into the ground pattern of regular unit sizes of paving or decking. Such formal shapes can really help to link the dimension and regular shapes of the house into the garden. With reliable modern materials water can be successfully contained and controlled in any form. Water pumps can be small and powerful and pond liners are now tough and have a long life expectancy. In the past, water in the garden was sometimes avoided as there was a fear of the pond leaking or the water pump breaking down, but these days the reliability of the materials means that water features can be built with confidence.

Having said that, the idea of bringing water and all the qualities that it holds to a city garden has to be carefully considered before any work is done. The introduction of water into a garden has many implications both aesthetically and practically. The first consideration is whether the addition of water will actually enhance the garden. This may seem a strange question, but people often install a water feature because it is expected rather than assessing whether it is going to be a valuable addition to the garden as a whole.

Water can be brought to a garden in many different forms from a small, wall-mounted feature, which re-circulates its own water, to a large pond or interconnecting ponds with water planting and fish, frogs or newts. Whatever the type of water feature you choose it's important that it is executed well and that it is maintained properly. If the water feature or pond is not maintained properly it will instantly deteriorate and detract from the look of the whole garden by looking messy. Think about maintenance before installing. Who will look after it and how long will it take to look after? A pond can be time consuming at particular times of the

year. These questions will help to decide the scale and type of water feature that is to be built.

Water can be introduced into the garden in many forms, from a pre-fabricated kit to an ambitious succession of waterfalls or fountains. Although there have been many advances in materials there is no denying that the more ambitious water projects can be problematic and do need careful consideration. Water is extremely heavy and will always find its own perfect level. The success through the construction of a larger or more complex pond or water feature will make it or break it. It is well worth employing a skilled landscaper to undertake the work.

Above: **The strong geometry of a circle works well when designing ponds in a city garden. To keep the water clear without filters it's important to achieve the right balance through planting.**

Wildlife

If desired, water will attract all forms of wildlife in the city whether it's a small feature used by birds as a bird bath or a pond colonised by a family of frogs or newts. Even within the city limits there is a diverse range of wildlife, which will be attracted by water and the life forms that are found both in and around ponds.

Sound

Sounds in a garden are difficult to create. However, the sounds of wind through the stems of a bamboo or the jangle of a wind chime are a couple of ways sound can be introduced into the garden. In the city, there are often background noises such as the hum of traffic or distant voices from a local bar or restaurant. It is difficult to drown out these noises completely, but the addition of even a small trickle will help to keep the focus within the garden. A more adventurous and larger-scale water feature may help to drown out louder sounds, but its size in relation to the garden has to be considered, even when dealing with an audible medium.

The sound of water will vary considerably depending on a variety of things. The shape of the spout or head of a fountain, the height from which the water falls and the depth of water it is falling into are just a few of the considerations which will affect the particular tone and pitch of the sound.

There are actually some water noises that can become rather irritating and can ruin a garden when switched on. A sound similar to a constant running tap or the loud noise of a violently gushing stream, which does not feel in proportion to a small city garden, certainly won't achieve the intended aim of adding a feeling of tranquillity to the outdoor room.

Hard landscaping

The construction of ponds and water features can be carried out in a variety of ways. Butyl liners are the most flexible and reliable. They can be bought

Opposite left: **The sheet of water created by this sculptural steel letterbox brings life and movement into a roof garden. This tall feature looks great even when the water is not running.**

Opposite right: **A simple copper pipe protruding through a wall makes a good waterspout. The all-important sound of water will vary considerably depending on the shape and height of the fountainhead.**

on a roll and used for awkward shapes or they can be 'box welded' and easily slipped into a pre-dug geometric shape. It is possible to build on top of a Butyl liner with concrete or cement to create steps or stepping stones. Concrete ponds can work successfully, but it is worth placing a liner underneath as a safety measure in case of any cracking. Pre-fabricated fibreglass liners are also available and in a variety of shapes. They can be the simplest and cheapest way to install a pond, but over time they will become brittle and possibly crack.

It is important to think about the edge of the pool with regard to how it will work with surrounding materials as well as how to disguise the liner. Evaporation in the summer will inevitably lead to the dropping of the water level, so make sure the construction compensates for the inner edge to be visible without the showing of any liner. This can be done by laying a course of stone or engineering brick below water level and on the inside face of the liner.

Reflective ponds

The reflective qualities of water will bring a special mood of calm to a garden, which cannot be achieved through any other medium. Perfectly still water, with its glass-like surface, creates a strong atmosphere in an outside space and any movement such as a light breeze or a leaf falling on it will make interesting ripple effects and add a subtle and ever-changing quality to the composition. The water surface may be intended to see only a reflection of the sky, which can look fantastic when looked down upon – as if it were a changing picture set into the garden.

The subject to be reflected should be considered carefully, as should the position from which it will be viewed. There may already be a particular composition in the garden that is ideal for reflecting in the water or maybe it's part of the overall design. If designing a garden from scratch a seating area could be considered so as to manipulate the direction from which the pond will be viewed.

The size, placing and type of construction of a reflective pond needs to

Opposite: **The proportion of a pond in relation to the rest of the garden is important. Painting the inside of a reflective pond a dark colour will give the best clarity to the reflection.**

119

be planned to maximise the visual effect of the water. The surface area, in particular, should be large enough to create the effect otherwise it will not draw the eye towards it successfully. It is important when constructing a pool like this that the water level comes up as high as possible to the edge. If there are a few inches between the top of the water and the top of the edge of the pond the reflection will appear to double the size of this line and therefore ruin the intended effect.

'It is always tempting to sit near to water, so think about building the pond at a perfect sitting height'

A big decision to make is whether the pool will be set into the ground or built up above ground level. Again, this all depends on what you want to see in it and from where you may want to see it. A raised pond will often create the opportunity to edge it with stone or tiles, which in turn can double up as seating in a garden. It is always tempting to sit near to water, so think about building the pond at a perfect sitting height, but be careful as if it's too high it may reduce the amount of surface that can be viewed.

To achieve the best reflective qualities from a pool it is important to make sure the bottom and edges are as dark as possible. Black will give the best clarity to a reflection, but other dark and interesting colours such as deep blues and purples can help to create exciting compositions.

Previous pages: **Modern concrete engineering can be applied to create ambitious and inspiring water gardens. This structure celebrates the essential qualities of water.**

Rills

A rill is a channel or man-made stream, which may link two ponds or the source of the rill and a pond. In a city garden they can work exceptionally well as they will add a subtle movement and intrigue to a garden. A rill will often sit comfortably in a city garden as the idea behind it is based on the deliberate manipulation of water. Small, concentrated quantities of water in a garden can sometimes feel out of proportion and have the effect of drawing the eye into a specific part of the garden. In contrast to this a rill will link spaces and lead you through the garden. The sound created by a rill will be understated and be a subtle addition to the garden. As with any form of moving water it is important to make sure the source or the head of the

Below: **A rill can help to link areas of a garden together. This stone walling makes a strong backdrop to the garden and could be quite imposing, but the addition of moving water helps to break it up whilst adding movement and sound to keep the garden alive.**

Above: **These slate tiles set into the wall at alternate angles are an imaginative way to make the flowing movement of the water more random, and in turn change the tone and feel of the sound created.**

Opposite: **Water should be introduced boldly and deliberately into the city garden. The blue of the walls, stream and iris flowers links the whole space together and makes for an integrated and harmonious design.**

rill fits in well with the whole scheme. A simple copper pipe or a half-rounded terracotta pipe emerging through a wall can be very effective. It also creates an opportunity to introduce some of your own personality into the garden. It's nice to find something particular to yourself, so maybe commission a sculptor whose work you particularly like to make something personal to you.

Another advantage of a rill is that it can be made with a very shallow depth of water and therefore there are few safety worries if you have small children. In fact, a rill is perfect for children to play with. Sailing walnut shell boats or leaves along a rill can keep children occupied for hours.

Wall-mounted water features

The easiest way to introduce the sound of water into a garden is to install a pre-fabricated wall-mounted water feature. These work by circulating their own water held in the lower reservoir and they generally come with a pre-installed pump and just need to be fixed to a wall and connected to the electrical supply. There are now many different types of wall-mounted water features on the market with a variety of finishes such as ceramic, terracotta, lead and fibreglass. The fibreglass ones can sometimes be made to imitate one of the other materials and can look pretty authentic.

These features can work really well in the very small garden as they will feel in proportion to the garden as a whole. With the limited space in a basement well or small backyard they can add the sound and movement of water without taking up a lot of space. They can also easily be fixed higher up the wall towards eye level and therefore help to draw the composition upwards into the whole of the space. It is a common problem in the small garden to have most of the interest at a low level, which will draw the eye downwards.

Waterfalls

Waterfalls can create some of the most dramatic and noisiest water features in a garden. In the contemporary city garden they can be a wall-mounted

Right: A single plant variety –
Zantedeschia aethiopica – makes
for a stunning display when in
flower. Water plays the role of
dividing the precise geometry of
squares within a square.

feature, which pours into a pond or a succession of ponds through which the water flows. The most important thing to consider when constructing a water feature is what will happen when the pump is switched off. This is why a waterfall or stream-like effect is, in fact, built as a succession of individual ponds, each holding their own water. When the pump is switched off, the water doesn't then all end up flowing to the bottom and overflowing the bottom pool. The lowest pool also needs to be the largest of the feature because otherwise, through the inevitable evaporation in the summer, the bottom pool would be empty before the top one is filled up.

The all-important movement of the water will depend on the actual material and size of the shelf over which the water will be pouring. Natural materials such as slate or stone can be used very effectively to create a sheet of water. If you are looking for a really wide sheet of water you will need to use a man-made material such as stainless steel set perfectly level to get an even flow over the entire length of the fall.

Fountains

Fountains can be added to a pond and give the flexibility of adding the sound and movement of water to an otherwise still pool. An underwater submersible pump will spray the water into the air and create movement and sound. There are different attachments available, which give a variety of effects from a single water jet to a fine spray, and they can easily be changed to keep the composition fresh. The movement of the water will also help to aerate the water for any fish.

Bubblejets

Bubblejets are a simple way of introducing water into a garden on the horizontal plane, either at ground level or incorporated into a raised bed. They work in a similar way to the wall-mounted features and add the sense and sound of water in a child-safe and understated way. With imagination, pre-fabricated kits can easily be customised to add a personal flavour to a garden while making the perfect birdbath.

'Visible plants in a city water garden should ideally be chosen for their leaf-shape and form as well as colour'

Planting

The planting of water gardens should be approached in a similar way to the planting of the garden as a whole. Simple repetition of selected plants rather than a collection of many varieties will give a more designed look. Furthermore, good planting will really help with the quality and clarity of water: dirty or cloudy water is not going to look good whatever style of garden.

Water plants are basically split into three groups – oxygenators, marginals and aquatics. Oxygenators are fully submersed and will really help to keep the water clear. Canadian pondweed (*Lagarosiphon major*), and *Ceratophyllum demersum* are two of the most reliable and quick spreading oxygenators. They generally come with small weights so they immediately sink to the bottom of a pond and quickly multiply.

Visible plants in a city water garden should ideally be chosen for their leaf-shape and form as well as colour. Marginals like to be planted in 2.5–18cm (1–6in) of water and aquatics between 25 and 66cm (10 and 26in), depending on the plant. Good marginals to use include *Typha minima*, which is a dwarf bulrush with a stiffly upright stem and strong simple outline that is just like the larger bulrush, but smaller. The arum lily, *Zantedeschia aethiopica*, is a reliable flowering stately plant that can be grown successfully as a bog plant or a marginal. It has an unmistakable and classic creamy white spathe in early summer.

Opposite: **A line of small bubblejets set within the shallow pool area plays with scale when set against the architectural nature of the spiky planting. A good filtration system is important to keep the water crystal clear.**

Sagittaria sagittifolia has the most elegant, arrow-shaped leaves and quickly forms dense clumps. The loose clusters of white three-petalled flowers appear as an added bonus in mid- to late summer. *Thalia dealbata* is a must with its striking lance-shaped foliage and tall panicles of purple flowers in mid- to late summer. It will easily grow to 2m (6ft) and helps add a sculptural form to a water garden.

The aquatic plants include the water hawthorn, *Aponogeton distachyos*, which is planted to a depth of up to 75cm (2½ft). Its dark green, long and oval leaves float on the surface of the water. The unusual forked white flower spikes have a strong vanilla fragrance. Another aquatic plant with leaves that float on the surface is the much-loved water lily. There is a water lily to suit every pond size and they come in a wide range of colours. They need quite a bit of sun to flower and prefer still water.

The balance of plants is essential in a pond to ensure good water quality. If there is no filtration system or regularly moving water it is important to plant the pond well. When the sun hits the surface of the water in spring it will encourage algae to grow, which turns the water green. All ponds will go a bit green in the spring, but if they are healthy they will quickly clear up. Covering the surface of a pond with plants will help keep the sunlight off the surface and therefore keep the water clear. Ideally, at least 50 per cent of the water surface should be covered, and this will also make hiding places for any fish.

Lighting

At night, the water garden can become a focal point for the whole garden. In larger ponds, the addition of a few underwater lights will make the entire surface of the water glow and bring a sense of mystery to the garden. If there are fish in the pond the lighting can make them look rather eerie and intriguing as they swim about.

Opposite: **The glassy surface of this pond reflects the sky as dusk falls. The relaxing mood that perfectly still water can bring to a garden makes the island summer house a great place to wind down after a busy day.**

Moving water such as a waterfall or bubblejet can be highlighted with a more specific light either set under the water level or hidden behind some planting near to the spout. This will help to emphasise the movement of the water in the dark, which would otherwise only be heard. Occasional lighting in the form of floating candles will add subtle movement to the garden at night.

Maintenance

The upkeep of a water feature or pond is critical to its success. Clear water is essential as it will always look good, and won't give off an unpleasant odour.

Bubblejets and the smaller wall-mounted features will need their water changing reasonably regularly as there is unlikely to be any aquatic plants present to help keep them clean. The easiest way is to utilise the existing pump by connecting a hose pipe on to it, and pump out the water down a rainwater drain. If there is a film of algae present in the reservoir tank it's worth scrubbing as much as possible of it off with warm soapy water before filling it back up. If there's a filter on the pump, take it off and thoroughly clean it before re-installing. U.V. filters are more expensive to install, but will keep the water crystal clear all year round.

A larger pond with plants shouldn't need to have its water changed. Aquatic plants grow vigorously so established ponds with plenty of planting will need to be thinned out about once a year. Spring is the best time to do this. If the plants are grown in baskets, lift and divide them by cutting through their rhizome and re-pot half of the plant as you would any other perennial in a pot. It is important to remove regularly any dead foliage that has fallen from trees and shrubs. Any rotting leaves will make the water smell and quickly ruin the all-important balance needed to ensure clean water.

Opposite: **The tall lush waterside planting of palms and bamboos helps to increase the privacy and makes this the perfect place to retreat from the city. Timber decks always look good when used next to water.**

the night garden

At night the city garden comes alive. On warm summer evenings there is nowhere better to relax, eat and entertain than in your garden. As the sun sets, what you have created as your outdoor space takes on a completely different look. The ability to extend the hours of your day into the garden can constitute the perfect antidote to stressful city living while reflecting urban culture and all that comes with it.

In fact, during a busy working week, the evening and night may be the only time you get to enjoy the outdoors. And at the weekend, the garden is the perfect place to forget about time. Relax in it during the day and experience the dusk slowly creeping in. Seamlessly the day and night are joined together.

In a warm summer, the garden can become the most important room in the house. It is the time of year when the most flexible of garden spaces can come into its own. It is a place where children can play safely into the evening and wear themselves out rather than get pent-up watching television. The terrace can become somewhere to cook and eat. It can be as if one is on a permanent holiday. Impromptu gatherings with friends and neighbours can just develop and the garden becomes the perfect place to party.

The winter garden has much to offer as well. One simple way of extending the use of the garden through the year might be the placing of a patio heater on the terrace. These gas-fired accessories are now available in smaller domestic sizes than the ones seen outside larger restaurants. They are very effective and make the notion of eating al fresco during the colder months perfectly realistic – as long as it isn't raining!

If well lit, a winter garden can continue to be a pleasure from indoors, in the form of a composition that is still seen and appreciated. There are times when garden lighting can be functional, dramatic and help to increase security all at the same time.

The liberating feeling of space in the city should, if possible, be exploited to its maximum. It is well worth planning lighting into the garden at an early stage to give the option of adding it later. Conduit pipes can be laid down under paths, walls or terraces during the construction works so that any electrical cabling can be fed through at a later date. In fact, lighting constitutes one of the most important factors when planning a night garden, whatever the time of year.

Creative lighting

Creative and imaginative garden lighting can transform any evening or night garden into a magical place. There are many techniques employed to create different lighting effects in a city garden. It is a whole new medium to be added to the garden and can be cleverly used to manipulate the garden by night. Certain elements such as plants, pots, water features or structural garden features can be emphasised, as can parts of the garden, which may not be so apparent by daylight. Indeed, entirely new compositions can be realised by the use of lighting. It may, as is often the case, be used just to

Previous pages: **During the summer the city garden becomes the perfect place to entertain. The** *Trachycarpus fortunei* **make a dramatic statement when lit from below, and the floating candles' flickering light adds movement to the stream.**

accent plants or features. Or subtle lighting of walls or steps helps to keep the strong layout of the city garden. This, in turn, will help to set off any structural planting. Exciting as it is, however, garden lighting should be used quite sparingly, as too many lights in a garden will simply wash the whole space with light and therefore the all-important definition will be lost.

Functional lighting

Lighting has functional qualities, which can be combined with creative lighting. Being able to see one's way around the garden at night may simply be practicable; also, safety is always important. It may, for example, be important to light any steps or paths you may have. This can be done by low-level lighting, which can also help to show the structure of the whole garden by night. Throwing pools of light on to terraces or eating areas can be achieved by placing a light high up on a house wall or in a tree to shine down on to a specific spot.

Lighting can also help with security, which is especially relevant in a city garden. Specific security lights set on sensors can become irritating as passing cats often sets them off. Pretty much any type of garden lighting will work as a deterrent. So, if possible, have the lights installed on two or three switches so that the lights can relate to the specific needs at the time.

LIGHTING TECHNIQUES
Spotlighting

Spotlighting is used specifically to highlight a particular plant or feature. It will create dramatic effects and will draw the eye towards whatever is being lit and therefore works well when viewed from a reasonable distance.

Uplighting

Uplighting is used to light the crown of a specific tree or large shrub. The light is set at ground level and points upwards to light the branches against

Below: **There are some interesting and well-designed candle holders on the market. Candle lighting is an affordable way to introduce light to the night garden and can keep the composition fresh.**

the night sky or dark background. This technique will help add height to a city garden. The lights should always face away from where the tree is to be viewed to avoid seeing the glare from the bulb.

Grazing

Grazing is mainly used as a technique to light walls or hard landscaping structures in a garden. The lights can be placed at an angle to show off a structure or surface such as the bricks in a brick wall or the slats of a fence. If the walls are painted it will bring colour into the night garden. Grazing walls with light will also help to keep the layout of a city garden at night; this is important if you don't want the garden to be overly 'soft' in its feel.

Downlighting

Downlighting can be either the lighting of the crown of a tree or lighting a specific area of garden from above. A series of lights set into the branches of a tree will imitate the effect of a strong moon and generally outline the shape of the tree. Downlighters set into a tree or fixed to a wall can be directed to create pools of light on specific areas of the garden to show the layout or certain features such as a path through an arch.

Underwater lighting

Waterproof lights can be placed under the water in ponds or fountains. These lights will give a glow to the water feature as a whole and emphasise any movement to the surface of the water. The underwater lighting of a waterfall or fountain can create a really dramatic effect and turn the waterfall into a cascade of light (see also 'The Water Garden').

Silhouetting and shadowing

Silhouetting is when a plant or sculpture is lit from the front specifically to cast a theatrical shadow on to a wall behind it. The shadow effect will

Opposite left: **Lighting can be dotted around to create a loose informal feel to the garden at night. The *Festuca glauca* grasses glow as they hold the light in their delicate leaves.**

Opposite right: **Uplighters on these bamboos add drama and movement to the outdoor space at night. The lighting also washes on to the red wall to introduce colour into the garden.**

Previous pages: **These individual and stunning specimens have been accented by picking out each one with an uplighter. The swimming pool has been lit with underwater lights so that it glows evenly across the surface to complete the composition.**

Opposite: **A variety of lighting has been used to bring this garden to life at night. The old brick wall on the right has been grazed with an angled light to highlight the relief. The tall shrubs at the back have been uplit to maintain the height in the planting.**

change according to the relative size of the object, as well as the placing and the power of the light. The light fitting should be hidden to achieve maximum effect.

Candle lighting

Candles give a delightful (and easily affordable) light to any garden and can create the right mood for anything, from an intimate dinner for two to the perfect party setting. There are many candleholders and lamps on the market that shield candles from the wind and give off a subtle flickering light, which has a living quality all of its own. Simple tea lights placed in a clear, white or coloured plastic cup can look great when placed in a line alongside a path or along the top of a wall. Candles stuck in sand at the bottom of a large paper bag (again any colour – brown paper looks good) can be both a fun and an imaginative way to introduce decorative lighting to a garden. The paper bag can have shapes such as stars cut into the sides, and be placed in a planting area or on each edge of a terrace to define the layout of the space.

'The great thing about occasional candle lighting is that it's not permanent and can be played around with to create different effects to keep the night garden looking fresh'

The great thing about occasional candle lighting is that it's not permanent and can be played around with to create different effects to keep the night garden looking fresh. One evening the candles can be placed in regimented lines to show off the strong structure of a garden and another night changed for a much looser feel.

Planting/scent

At all times of the year, scent in a city garden can evoke certain moods and stimulate the mind. Heady aromas can trigger memories and help transport you to a different place. In the evening and at night, however, scent can become more important than the visual qualities of the plant and are critical to the garden experience. For this reason, it is important to remember to plant scented plants where they can create the most effect. This will generally be around seating areas or near to the back door of the house or apartment. There are many winter and early spring flowering scented plants but, of course, if you don't venture into the garden during this time of year the scent will be lost. It is usually the summer flowering scented plants that are mostly worth considering planting in a small garden for night scent. Plants which flower during the spring or winter months can be planted in areas where they will be appreciated at this time of year such as front gardens, where they cannot be missed.

Pittosporum tobira is a Meditteranean-looking evergreen with large glossy leaves. Its clusters of creamy white flowers have a heavenly scent in mid-summer. For the smaller garden go for *P. tobira* 'Nanum', which only reaches 1m (3ft), or 'Variegatum', which has grey-green leaves with a white edge and is much slower growing.

Abelia x *grandiflora* is a graceful, arching evergreen shrub reaching 1m (3ft) and has scented white and pink tinged flowers. It will flower from mid- to late summer. *Euphorbia mellifera* has large clusters of yellow-green and red honey-scented flowers, which seem to hold on till late spring, especially to be enjoyed.

Climbers such as jasmines and honeysuckles are reliable and will always be good value as far as introducing scent into a garden. Grown over an arch to be walked through or on a pergola over a seating area is a good way of making sure the scent is not lost. *Trachelospermum jasminoides* has a sweet-scented white flower on a tidy evergreen climber, which is clothed to the ground in leaves.

Opposite: **The strong light on the white walls shows off the plants in silhouette and is bounced back into the seating area. Interesting shadows are thrown onto the ceiling to help define the space.**

Aromatic foliage

It is not only the flowers of a plant that may be scented. Aromatic foliage can be surprisingly pungent. Lavender and rosemary are unbeatable for filling the night garden with an unmistakable Mediterranean scent. There are other herbs which have aromatic foliage and can be picked and thrown straight on to the barbecue. Fennel is a beautiful garden plant, which can reach over 2m (6ft) and therefore helps add real height as well as an aniseed scent. Sage is easy to grow in a pot or over the wall of a raised planter. The evergreen purple sage always looks great cascading over a wall and is easy to grow.

Plant form and texture

When lighting specific plants, it is the form and texture that will add a personal touch to the garden. Wispy plants such as the taller grasses or frothy plants like *Verbena bonariensis* will both filter and hold the light in their delicate form. More solid plants such as box or bay will help to formalise a space when lit, but can make the garden look a bit stodgy if there is no textural contrast with lighter forms.

To add both drama and movement to a garden, cast shadows on to walls by night lighting. Garden structures and plants can both be lit from a specific angle to throw an intriguing shape on to a chosen wall. The larger-leaved plants such as a fig or a fatsia will create an original composition when cast on to a wall by a strategically placed light. A light wind on these plants will add a simple movement to the night garden and keep the space alive.

The bark of a small tree such as a silver birch or the copper-red peeling bark of *Prunus serrula* can look great and add real drama when picked out by a single light. It will draw the eye towards a feature of the plant that may not be so distinct by day and help to see the garden in a whole new light.

Pages 146–7: **Lighting can successfully link the interior to the exterior. The functional lighting under the spiral staircase both increases safety and highlights the coloured wall.**

Left: **These Mexican blue palms** *Brahea armata* **look great when lit from beneath through a metal grille with a blue fluorescent light, and make a really contemporary composition.**

plant directory

TREES

Trees will help to structure a garden and add height. A well-placed tree will increase privacy or cast shade where it's needed.

Acacia dealbata
(silver wattle/mimosa)

This fast growing evergreen tree is best grown as a single specimen. It has particularly fine foliage with its fern-like, feathery, blue-green leaves. The pleasant and strongly scented yellow pompom flowers completely cover the tree in early spring. They are much hardier than is generally thought, but may die back in an extremely harsh winter.
Height x spread 9 x 6m (30 x 20ft) after 10 years
Prefers full sun
Hardy to -13°C when established

Acer palmatum 'Bloodgood'

One of the finest of the slow growing maples, it makes a perfect tree for the sheltered small garden. Its habit is more slender and upright than other varieties. The rich purple, finely cut foliage adds colour throughout the summer and then turns a dramatic deep red in autumn. Plant in a sheltered spot as a single specimen tree or in a group as the perfect backdrop.

Height x spread 5 x 2.5m (16 x 8ft) after 10 years
Partial shade
Hardy to -23°C

Arbutus unedo (strawberry tree)

This slow growing upright evergreen tree or large shrub will add a sculptural quality to the garden. The dark green leaves show off the clusters of delicate white bell-shaped flowers, which appear in late summer and turn into strawberry-like fruits in the autumn. It can be clipped to shape when necessary, or prune back the lower branches to expose the added bonus of its cinnamon-brown bark.
Height x spread 3 x 2.5m (10 x 8ft) after 10 years
Will tolerate some shade
Hardy to -13°C

Betula utilis var. jacquemontii

This graceful and deciduous tree works well with modern architecture and garden designs. The nearly pure white peeling bark can almost single-handedly carry a garden composition through the winter. They are available in single or multi-stemmed specimens and can easily be underplanted as they don't cast much shade.
Height x spread 10 x 4m

(33 x 13ft) after 10 years
Full sun to light shade
Hardy to -35°C

Catalpa bignonioides
(Indian bean tree)

The large, aromatic, pale-green leaves and spreading habit make it perfect to help shade a sunny terrace. The flowers are white and foxglove-like and are followed by long black pods.
Height x spread 8 x 9m (26 x 30ft) after 10 years
Sun
Hardy to -20°C

Cercis siliquastrum (Judas tree)

This unusual, slow growing tree has purple flowers on the main trunk as well as on its branches before it comes into leaf. Its leaves are rounded, and turn yellow in autumn.
Height x spread 3 x 3m (10 x 10ft) after 10 years
Full sun
Hardy to -17°C

Ficus carica (fig)

The gnarled twisted form of this small tree combined with the large, green, indented leaf makes it a very useful tree in a small garden. Perfect to shade a sunny terrace. It can be left

to spread in its free-form manner or trained against a warm wall where it is more likely to produce its delicious fruit in cooler areas.
Height x spread 4.5 x 4.5m (15 x 15ft) after 10 years
Fruits best in full sun
Hardy to -7°C

Magnolia grandiflora (bull bay)

Can be grown as a tree or trained against a wall. Looks stately when grown on the corner of an imposing building or symmetrically on either side of an entrance. The large, glossy, evergreen leaves have a felty, cinnamon underside, and the large, creamy yellow, bowl-shaped flowers are highly scented and are an added bonus from summer through to autumn.
Height x spread 4 x 1.8m (13 x 6ft) after 10 years
Flowers best in a sunny sheltered position, but will tolerate some shade
Magnolia grandiflora 'Edith Bogue' – hardy to -18°C
Magnolia grandiflora 'Exmouth' – hardy to -23°C

Olea europaea (olive)

The evergreen grey-green foliage combined with its crooked habit makes the olive a great tree for the city garden. Hardier than generally thought, it combines well with other silver or grey foliage plants, or does well in a large pot as a focal point on a roof terrace or courtyard garden.
Height x spread 4 x 3m (13 x 10ft) after 10 years
Full sun
Hardy to -7°C

Prunus x subhirtella 'Autumnalis' (winter flowering cherry)

An exquisite small deciduous tree for a city and town garden. Its clusters of semi-double white flowers in late winter and early spring will bring much-needed joy towards the end of a long winter. Its delicate habit when in leaf won't shade or dominate a city garden. Ideal for either the front or back garden.
Height x spread 4 x 3m (13 x 10ft) after 10 years
Will tolerate shade
Hardy to -23°C

Pyrus salicifolia 'Pendula' (willow-leaved pear)

Its neat weeping habit and willow-like grey leaves make this a good tree for the city garden. It is slow growing, will stay small and is easily controlled. Eventually it will be as wide as it is tall and works well as a single specimen in a front garden or planted in symmetry.
Height x spread 3 x 3m (10 x 10ft) after 10 years
Full sun
Hardy to -29°C

Pyrus salicifolia

Robinia pseudoacacia 'Frisia' (false acacia)

The cultivar 'Frisia' is smaller than the standard *R. pseudoacacia*, which with its pollution tolerance makes it a good tree for the city. Its mophead of feathery golden flowers will add a strong colour into the garden and help to break up a mid-green composition or contrast well with tall red-brick walls.
Height x spread 6 x 4m (20 x 13ft) after 10 years
Full sun
Hardy to -29°C

Taxus baccata (yew)

In a city garden, the yew is best used as a hedge or topiary piece. It can be pruned back and grown into almost any shape to create a great backdrop, divide or single specimen. Slow growing at first, but once established helps enormously with the structural planting of a garden. Seeds are very poisonous.
Height x spread 2 x 1.6m
(6½ x 5ft) after 10 years
Can tolerate deep shade
Hardy to -23°C

SHRUBS

Shrubs are the backbone of a planting scheme. Choose shrubs for structure and year-round interest for a city garden.

Buxus sempervirens (box)

The perfect evergreen for clipping into low hedges and topiary shapes to help formalise a city garden. It's slow growing and has small, glossy, mid-green leaves. Depending on the style of the garden it can be kept extremely neat or left a bit looser.
Height x spread 1.5 x 1.5m
(4 x 4ft) after 10 years
Sun or shade
Hardy to -23°C

Choisya ternata
(Mexican orange blossom)

A commonly grown, but still useful, evergreen shrub with aromatic glossy leaves. Its sweetly scented white flowers appear in spring, and then a second flush will appear in autumn. Makes a good informal hedge.
Height x spread 2 x 2m (6 x 6ft)
after 10 years
Sun or shade
Hardy to -15°C

Convolvulus cneorum (silver bush)

The silky and silvery leaves of this small evergreen shrub look as if they have been sprayed with a spray paint. The large, white, pink tinged flowers are produced all summer long. This is a very good plant for breaking up the line of a raised bed.
Height x spread 45 x 75cm
(1½ x 2½ft) after 10 years
Full sun
Hardy to -12°C

Cornus alba 'Sibirica Variegata'
(red-barked dogwood)

A useful plant with all-year-round interest. The crimson red stems in winter look stunning against a foliage backdrop or coloured wall when grown en masse. This variegated variety has creamy-white edges to the leaves, which can help lift a composition.
Height x spread 2.5 x 4m (8 x 13ft)
after 10 years
Will tolerate light shade
Hardy to -40°C

Cotinus coggygria 'Royal Purple'
(smoke bush)

The purple leaves of this deciduous shrub will add a bold colour to the city garden. It works well with many different colours, including yellows, greys and greens. Smoky plume-like flowers appear in summer and last till the autumn when the foliage turns a bright red.
Height x spread 2 x 2m (6 x 6ft)
after 10 years
Prefers sun
Hardy to -29°C

Euphorbia characias subsp. wulfenii (spurge)

This evergreen forms a loose dome of pale grey-green leaves. Its tall, sculptural, acid-yellow flowers appear in early spring, and last till early summer. They create a dramatic effect in the small garden, but be careful of the milky white sap as it is an irritant.
Height x spread 1.5 x 1.5m
(5 x 5ft) after 10 years
Sun or shade
Hardy to -12°C

Fatsia japonica

The large glossy leaves and its tolerance of shade make this evergreen plant ideal for many a city setting. The added bonus of its unusual creamy-white globular flowers appears in autumn. It makes a great backdrop to a garden

and works well with modern
buildings.
Height x spread 3.5 x 4.5m
(12 x 15ft) after 10 years
Sun to heavy shade
Hardy to -12°C

Lavandula angustifolia (lavender)
A robust, dome-shaped shrub with
excellent foliage, flower and scent.
The grey-green leaves and blue
flower spikes work well with a wide
variety of plants. Grows well in a
pot or as a low hedge to border
paths. 'Hidcote' is a more compact
form with deep purple coloured
flowers.
Height x spread 80 x 80cm
(2½ x 2½ft) after 10 years
Full sun
Hardy to -23°C

Nandina domestica 'Firepower'
(sacred bamboo)
Grown mainly for its delicate
foliage, which is reddish purple
when young turning to a brighter
red in autumn and winter. This
plant has large sprays of starry
white flowers in summer followed
by red berries. It looks good when
planted by itself in front of a wall
as a single specimen or when used
in a group.
Height x spread 1.2m x 60cm
(4 x 2ft) after 10 years
Sunny and sheltered
Hardy to -12°C

Osmanthus delavayi
Compact, dome-shaped, evergreen
plants with small, dark green glossy
leaves and small, white, scented,
tubular-shaped flowers in spring.
Good for the front garden. They can
be pruned as an effective low
hedge.
Height x spread 1.6 x 2m (5 x 6ft)
after 10 years
Sun or shade
Hardy to -12°C

Phormium tenax
(New Zealand flax)
A tall architectural evergreen with
sword-shaped leaves, which can add
dramatic height to a small garden.
It is a good plant as a focal point
or to help increase screening or
privacy.
Height x spread 2 x 1m (6 x 3ft)
after 10 years
Prefers full sun
Hardy to -12°C

Photinia x fraseri 'Red Robin'
A solid evergreen plant. Its sharp-
toothed foliage is a bright intense
red when young, and turns a glossy
green in summer. It works extremely
well when planted in quantity as a
backdrop to a city garden and is
virtually maintenance free.
Height x spread 2 x 2m (6 x 6ft)
after 5 years
Sun or shade
Hardy to -18°C

Pittosporum tobira
A large bushy evergreen, it can be
grown in containers, as a single
specimen or as a hedge. The dark,
glossy, oblong leaves will add a
lush feel to a border, and the
creamy white flowers in summer
will fill a small garden with their
heady scent.
Height x spread 3 x 3m (10 x 10ft)
after 10 years
Good in sun or shade
Hardy to -12°C

Prunus laurocerasus 'Otto Luyken'
A good dense evergreen with erect
and upward growing stems, which
are covered in small white flowers
in mid-spring. It is useful to grow
in quantity as a dense ground cover
in shady areas and around the base
of trees.
Height x spread 1 x 1m (3 x 3ft)
after 10 years
Sun or shade
Hardy to -18°C

Rosmarinus officinalis 'Miss
Jessopp's Upright' (rosemary)
More than just a herb, rosemary is
a great evergreen garden plant. Its
aromatic, dark green, needle-like
leaves are covered with clusters of
blue flowers in summer. This variety
is very upright in its habit and can
be clipped into a semi-formal
hedge. Its aroma is best
appreciated near a seating area.

Clematis 'Etoile Violette'

Height x spread 1 x 1m (3 x 3ft)
after 10 years
Full sun
Hardy to -12°C

Viburnum plicatum 'Mariesii'

The horizontal spreading habit and
the white flower clusters on the
top of the tiered branches make
this a showy specimen plant for a
small garden. It is a slow growing
deciduous plant with deep veined
leaves that turn a rich, reddish

purple. The lower branches can be
pruned to turn it into a small tree.
Height x spread 3 x 4m (10 x 13ft)
after 10 years
Sun or shade
Hardy to -20°C

Yucca gloriosa (Adam's needle)

The sharp, sword-like, rigid leaves
make up the architectural form of this
accent plant. The 2m (6ft) high
flowers are stunning, but you may
need to wait five years before they
appear. 'Variegata' has leaves edged
and striped with creamy yellow. Plant
out of reach of children.
Height x spread 1 x 1m (3 x 3ft)
after 10 years
Full sun
Hardy to -18°C

CLIMBERS

In a city garden there are often
plenty of opportunities to grow
climbing plants, whether it's to
cover a wall or fence, or to grow
over a structure to increase privacy
or create shade.

Clematis armandii

A lush looking evergreen climber
with large, finger-like, leathery
leaves. Its strongly vanilla-scented
creamy-white flowers appear in
spring and will grow and flower
well in shade. Has a tendency to
get straggly. Prune off old brown
leaves to keep it looking neat.

Height 6m (20ft) after 10 years
Sun or shade
Hardy to -12°C

Clematis 'Etoile Violette'

A deciduous climber grown for its
beautifully rich violet purple
flowers, which appear in late
summer to autumn. It is great for
a splash of colour late in the
season.
Height 3.5m (12ft) after 3 years
Sun – keep roots in shade
Hardy to -29°C

Hedera canariensis 'Gloire de Marengo' (Canary Island ivy)

The variegated, white-edged and
grey-green centred leaves will
really lift a dark shady wall and
create a good backdrop for other
planting. As it is an evergreen self-
clinging climber, it will find its
own way up walls and fences and
needs almost no maintenance.
Height 9m (30ft) after 5 years
Sun or shade
Hardy to -12°C

Humulus lupulus 'Aureus' (golden hop)

This very fast herbaceous climber
has a bright, golden-yellow, palmate
leaf. It can really help to visually lift
a dark wall.
Height 5m (16ft) after 5 years
Sun
Hardy to -29°C

Jasminum officinale
(common jasmine)

The unmistakable heavenly scent of the jasmine will instantly make you feel like you are on holiday! Although a rather untidy deciduous climber it will flower reliably in any aspect. Thin it out after flowering to keep it under control.
Height 3m (12ft) after 5 years
Sun or shade
Hardy to -18°C

Parthenocissus henryana

Useful deciduous climber to cover a wall or fence. The bluey-white veins on the leaf enhance the dark green velvety leaves, making an interesting textural backdrop to a garden. The leaves turn a spectacular and eye-catching red in autumn.
Height 3.5m (13ft) after 5 years
Sun or shade
Hardy to -18°C

Trachelospermum jasminoides
(evergreen jasmine)

A neat evergreen climber clothed to the ground with small, slender, dark-green leaves. It needs warm summers, so doesn't thrive in cooler climates. Its small white flowers are strongly jasmine scented and will fill a small garden in summer. It is a lot more shade tolerant than commonly thought and is easy to keep under control. Better on a wall than on a pergola.
Height 5m (16ft) after 10 years
Sun or shade – will lose its leaves in a cold winter
Hardy to -7°C

Vitis coignetiae
(crimson glory vine)

The huge leaves (up to 30cm [1ft] long) turn a spectacular shade of orange, red and crimson in the autumn. A vigorous plant, it is best grown over a structure or to hide a garden shed.
Height 5m (16ft) after 5 years
(ultimately 25m [80ft])
Sun or partial shade
Hardy to -29°C

Wisteria sinensis

When in flower, the wisteria has to be the most stunning of the climbing plants. It is best grown against a wall or over a pergola where the fragrant violet-blue flowers can hang free like big bunches of grapes. Regular pruning is necessary to produce plenty of flowers and to keep it a manageable size.
Height 10m (30ft) after 10 years
Full sun
Hardy to -29°C

PERENNIALS

These increase the palette of textures and colours in the city garden. Some perennials can be grown as effective ground cover to suppress weeds.

Acanthus mollis Latifolius Group
(bear's breeches)

Both the foliage and the flower make this a statuesque plant. The handsome, luxuriant leaves are lobed and can reach up to 75cm (2½ft) long. A white bloom and purplish bract combine to form a distinctive flower, which will add a striking vertical accent to the garden.
Height x spread 1.2 x 1.2m
(4 x 4ft)
Sun or light shade
Hardy to -12°C

Agave americana (century plant)

Succulent tropical perennial with stiff, spiky, blue-grey, sword-shaped leaves. As it is a strong, architectural-shaped plant it looks best when kept clear or lining a path in pots. Cut off the sharp spikes and keep away from children. They will need winter protection in cold areas.
Height x spread 1 x 1m (3 x 3ft)
after 5 years
Full sun
Hardy to -5°C

Ajuga reptans (bugle)

An evergreen perennial with a low growing carpeting habit that makes

Allium hollandicum 'Purple Sensation'

it an excellent ground cover. There are many varieties with green through to purple and bronze leaves. They generally have short blue flower spikes in early summer.
Height 10–20cm (4–8in)
Sun or shade
Hardy to -34°C

Alchemilla mollis (lady's mantle)
A reliable plant that is easy to grow in most situations. The lime-green, frothy flowers and pale grey-green leaves will work well in large clumps in any scheme or as the ideal filler plant.

Height x spread 80 x 45cm
(30 x 18in)
Sun or shade
Hardy to -34°C

Allium hollandicum 'Purple Sensation'
The dark purple and almost perfectly spherical flowerheads appear in early summer as the strap-like leaves wither away. They look excellent mixed with other perennials and grasses and are very easy to grow.
Height 75cm (2½ft)
Full sun
Hardy to -34°C

Crocosmia 'Lucifer' (montbretia)
Sword-shaped leaves and an eye-catching fiery red tropical flower. It will start flowering in mid- to late summer and will continue into the autumn.
Height 1.2m (4ft)
Full sun
Hardy to -29°C

Epimedium x versicolor 'Sulphureum' (bishop's mitre)
An excellent, semi-evergreen, carpeting ground cover for shade. Its heart-shaped leaves are reddish purple in spring and turn a bronze in autumn. The delicate yellow flowers on long spurs are perfectly fitting for spring.
Height 30cm (12in)

Full or semi-shade
Hardy to -18°C

Eryngyium bourgatii 'Oxford Blue'
A real spiky number. The deeply cut grey-green leaves have a striking silver vein. The rounded, steely-blue, thistle-like flowerheads are borne on similar coloured stems. The flower and the leaf work really well together to form an excellent garden plant.
Height x spread 60 x 50cm
(2 x 1½ft)
Sun
Hardy to -29°C

Euphorbia amygdaloides var. robbiae (Mrs Robb's bonnet)
One of the best evergreen ground-cover plants for shade. Its dark green leaves set off the acid yellow flowers in spring, and will help to lift a shady garden. It's a good spreader so let it fill a space without competition.
Height x spread 45 x 45cm
(18 x 18in)
Sun or shade
Hardy to -12°C

Foeniculum vulgare 'Purpureum' (bronze fennel)
Although a delicious herb, it is also a beautiful garden plant that will combine well with most colours. The delicate, feathery, bronze

foliage will tower up to 2m (6ft) in mid-summer. The flowers are hazy yellow and will self-seed if left.
Height x spread 2m x 60cm (6 x 2ft)
Sun
Hardy to -39°C

Helleborus orientalis
(Lenten rose)

Flowers from winter through to spring in varying shades of white, pale pink through to plum spotted with maroon. It can be used as an effective ground cover and needs to be planted in quantity where it will be seen during the winter months. Seeds freely.
Height x spread 45 x 60cm
(1½ x 2ft)
Shade
Hardy to -39°C

Hosta 'Halcyon' (plantain lily)

This silver-blue-leaved hosta is one of the finest. The sumptuous and architectural foliage of hostas will add a cool calm to the garden on a hot day. They work well in containers where they may be safer from the dreaded slugs and snails!
Height x spread 50cm x 1m
(1½ x 3ft)
Best in dappled shade
Hardy to -40°C

Ligularia 'The Rocket'

The tall, yellow, flower spikes on a thin black stem make a dramatic composition against a dark green foliage backdrop or wall. The leaves are large triangles with a serrated edge. Needs plenty of moisture.
Height x spread 1.8 x 1m (6 x 3ft)
Partial shade
Hardy to -34°C

Macleaya cordata (plume poppy)

A tall, majestic plant that rarely

Helleborus orientalis

needs staking. Its strong, grey-green, serrated, heart-shaped leaves are the perfect foil for the frothy, cream, plume-like flowers.
Height x spread 2m x 60cm (6 x 2ft)
Prefers full sun
Hardy to -34°C

Melianthus major

Large, blue, serrated leaves give this

plant a dramatic, sculptural value in the garden. The foliage is deeply cut and looks best when grown as a single specimen for a focal point.
Height x spread 2.4 x 2m (8 x 6ft)
Sun
Hardy to -6ºC

Pachysandra terminalis 'Variegata'
A very useful spreading evergreen ground cover, which will grow in the shade of trees and shrubs. The variegated leaf will help to lighten up a dark area all year round.
Height 15cm (6in)
Sun or shade
Hardy to -29ºC

Rheum palmatum
(Chinese rhubarb)
The large deeply cut rhubarb-like leaves make this one of the most architectural and dramatic perennial plants. Excellent as a single specimen or even better en masse if there's enough space. Needs plenty of moisture.
Height x spread 1.2 x 1.5m
(4 x 5ft)
Semi shade
Hardy to -28ºC

Salvia officinalis 'Purpurascens'
The decorative purple-leaved variety of the common sage, and just as delicious. It's a good evergreen garden plant, will work with a variety of colours and looks

best when left to scramble over a low retaining wall or grown in a pot.
Height x spread 60 x 45cm
(24 x 18in)
Full sun
Hardy to -23ºC

Verbena bonariensis
(purple top)
The sprays of small purple flowers on tall, delicate, almost invisible stems make this a winner with all types of planting. Their loose habit can help break up a stodgy planting scheme. Plants often die in winter, but replace themselves with self-sown seedlings.
Height x spread 1m x 60cm
(3 x 2ft)
Full sun
Hardy to -6ºC

PALMS
Palms are architectural in nature and can be used as excellent specimen plants.

Brahea armata
(Mexican blue palm)
Classic, fan-shaped leaves of a stunning steely-blue colour. It will need protection through the winter when young, but can withstand temperatures down to -10ºC. When larger, it will do much better in the ground than in a pot.
Height x spread 3 x 2m (10 x 6ft)
after 10 years

Full sun
Hardy to -10ºC

Cordyline australis
(cabbage palm)
The architectural form of this palm-like evergreen can be used in a wide variety of ways in the city garden, such as an accent plant, in a mixed scheme or in a formal garden. They are good for the roof garden as they do well in containers and can tolerate wind.
Height x spread 2.4 x 2m
(8 x 6½ft) after 10 years
Sun or shade – protect in a cold winter
Hardy to -7ºC

Musa basjoo (hardy banana)
Not strictly a palm, but its enormous fresh green leaves will add a tropical flavour to any garden. It does well in the protection of most city gardens. It doesn't mind sun or shade, but hates the wind, which will rip its delicate leaves.
Height x spread 2.4 x 1.5m (8 x 5ft)
Sun or shade – protect trunk from frosts
Hardy to -7ºC

Phoenix canariensis
(Canary Island date palm)
A vase-shaped, dark-green palm that will quickly develop a trunk. It is one of the easiest palms to grow

and will look good either in a pot on the terrace or planted in rows. It makes for an unusual hedge.
Height x spread 4 x 2m (12 x 6ft) after 10 years
Prefers full sun, but will tolerate some shade
Hardy to -7ºC

Trachycarpus fortunei (Chusan palm)

The hardiest of palms with a classic palm-shaped silhouette. The fibrous trunk will quickly develop to create a tall, majestic upright palm. It can tolerate wind, even though its fronds may droop, so it makes a good plant for the roof terrace.
Height x spread 12 x 3m (40 x 10ft)
Sun or light shade
Hardy to -15ºC

BAMBOOS

Bamboos will add height and movement to a small garden without too much width.

Fargesia murieliae

A particularly elegant specimen, the narrow slender stems have tapered leaves and will add a sense of movement to any garden. They are clump forming and fast growing.
Height x spread 3 x 1m (10 x 3ft)
Sun or light shade
Hardy to -34ºC

Phyllostachys nigra (black bamboo)

The green stems quickly turn black, and make this a great plant for a city garden. They add a strong vertical movement and have a wide variety of uses including screening and increasing privacy. They can be grown in pots, but need regular feeding and plenty of water.
P. aurea is the golden bamboo. Its pale green canes turn a golden-yellow.
Height x spread 3.5 x 1m (13 x 3ft) after 10 years
Sun or light shade
Hardy to -23ºC

Pleioblastus variegatus

A low growing bamboo with white, striped, variegated leaves. It is perfect for the small garden and looks best when planted by itself in bold blocks. It can be grown in a container, but will need plenty of water.
Height x spread 1 x 1.2m (3 x 4ft)
Sun or light shade
Hardy to -23ºC

GRASSES

These plants will add texture and movement to the modern garden.

Calamagrostis x acutiflora 'Karl Foerster' (feather reed grass)

Silvery-purple, stiff, upright leaves make this a useful vertical form when combining with other plants. The hazy flowerheads start off pink and turn yellow in autumn.
Height x spread 2 x 1m (6 x 3ft)
Full sun
Hardy to -29ºC

Festuca glauca (blue fescue)

This small, grey-blue, evergreen grass is extremely versatile. It keeps its neat shape well and can be used to punctuate planting, or looks great when grown in pots.
Height x spread 30 x 30cm (1 x 1ft)
Sun
Hardy to -34ºC

Trachycarpus fortunei

dangerous plants

Here is a list of plants which are often found in, or are available for planting in, gardens. It describes three types of potential risk.

EXTERNAL EFFECTS AS

1. **Skin irritants**
2. **Eye irritants**

INTERNAL EFFECTS AS

3. **Poisons**

The poisons category includes plants known to present any level of hazard. When eaten, some may cause mild illness, and a very few may cause severe poisoning. The correct approach is to avoid eating any plants listed as poisonous.

Aconite: See *Aconitum*

Aconitum: poisonous; skin irritant

Aesculus: poisonous

Agrostemma githago: poisonous

Alstroemeria: skin irritant

Angel's trumpet: see *Brugmansia*

Aquilegia: poisonous

Arum: poisonous; skin and eye irritant

Atropa: poisonous; skin irritant

Brugmansia: poisonous

Buckthorn: see *Rhamnus*

Burning bush: see *Dictamnus*

Caladium: poisonous

Caltha: poisonous; skin and eye irritant

Castor oil plant: see *Ricinus*

Catharanthus rosens: poisonous

Cherry laurel: see *Prunus laurocerasus*

Chincherinchee: see *Ornithogalum*

Christmas cherry: see *Solanum*

Chrysanthemum: see *Dendranthema*

Colchicum: poisonous

Columbine: see *Aquilegia*

Convallaria majalis: poisonous

x *Cupressocyparis leylandii*: skin irritant

Daffodil: see *Narcissus*

Daphne: poisonous; skin irritant

Datura: poisonous; skin irritant

Datura, tree: see *Brugmansia*

Delphinium (inc. *Consolida*): poisonous

Dendranthema: skin irritant

Dictamnus: skin irritant

Dieffenbachia: poisonous; skin and eye irritant

Digitalis: poisonous

Dumb cane: see *Dieffenbachia*

Echium: skin irritant

Euonymus: poisonous

Euphorbia: poisonous; skin and eye irritant

NB *Poinsettia* does not present a serious hazard

Ficus carica: skin and eye irritant

Foxglove: see *Digitalis*

Frangula: see *Rhamnus*

Fremontodendron: skin and eye irritant

Gaultheria: poisonous

Giant hogweed: see *Heracleum mantegazzianum*

Gloriosa superba: poisonous

Glory lily: see *Gloriosa*

Hedera: poisonous; skin irritant

Helleborus: poisonous; skin irritant

Henbane: see *Hyoscyamus*

Heracleum mantegazzianum: severe skin irritant in bright sunlight

Hyacinthus: skin irritant

Hyoscyamus: poisonous

Ipomoea: poisonous

Iris: poisonous; skin irritant

Ivy: see *Hedera*

Juniperus sabina: poisonous

Kalmia: poisonous

Laburnum: poisonous

Lantana: poisonous; skin irritant

Larkspur: see *Delphinium*

Laurel: see *Prunus*

Lily of the valley: see *Convallaria*

Ligustrum: poisonous

Lobelia (except bedding lobelia): poisonous; skin and eye irritant

Lupinus: poisonous

Madagascar periwinkle: see *Catharanthus*

Marsh marigold: see *Caltha*

Monkshood: see *Aconitum*

Morning glory: see *Ipomoea*

Narcissus: poisonous; skin irritant

Nerium oleander: poisonous

Nightshade, deadly: see *Atropa*

Nightshade, woody: see *Solanum*

Oleander: see *Nerium*

Ornithogalum: poisonous; skin irritant

Pernettya: see *Gaultheria*

Phytolacca: poisonous; skin irritant

Poinsettia: see *Euphorbia*

Pokeweed: see *Phytolacca*

Polygonatum: poisonous

Primula obconica: skin irritant

Privet: see *Ligustrum*

Prunus laurocerasus: poisonous

Rhamnus (including *Frangula*): poisonous; skin irritant

Rhus verniciflua, R. radicans, R. succedanea: poisonous; severe skin irritant

Ricinus communis: poisonous

Rue: see *Ruta*

Ruta: severe skin irritant in bright sunlight

Schefflera: skin irritant

Solandra: poisonous

Solanum (most species): poisonous

Solomon's seal: see *Polygonatum*

Spindle tree: see *Euonymus*

Spurge: see *Euphorbia*

Sumach: see *Rhus*

Taxus: poisonous

Thornapple: see *Datura*

Thuja: poisonous; skin irritant

Tulipa: skin irritant

Veratrum: poisonous

Wisteria: poisonous

Yew: see *Taxus*

suppliers

PLANT NURSERIES

Apple Court Nursery
Hordle Lane
Hordle
Lymington
Hampshire SO41 0HU
Tel 01590 642130
Fax 01590 644220
E-mail applecourt@btinternet.com
Website www.applecourt.com
Ferns, grasses and hostas.

Architectural Plants
Cooks Farm
Nuthurst
Horsham
West Sussex RH13 6LH
Tel 01403 891772
Fax 01403 891056
E-mail architecturalplants@
horsham.intelynx.net

Ausfern Nurseries
Kinglea Plant Centre
Sedge Green
Nazeing
Essex EN9 2PA
Tel 01992 465073
Fax 01992 465074
E-mail ausfern@attglobal.net
New Zealand plants including tree-ferns.

The Citrus Centre
Marehill Nursery
West Mare Lane
Pulborough
West Sussex RH20 2EA
Tel 01789 872786
Fax 01798 874880
E-mail enquiries@citruscentre.co.uk
Website www.citruscentre.co.uk

Hoecroft Plants
Severals Grange
Holt Road
Wood Norton
Dereham
Norfolk NR20 5BL
Tel 01362 684206
Fax 01362 684206

Langley Boxwood Nurseries
Rake
Liss
Hants GU33 7JL
Tel 01730 894467
Fax 01730 894703
E-mail langbox@msn.com
Website www.boxwood.co.uk
50 varieties of box available.
Topiary pieces.

The Palm Centre
Ham Central Nursery
Ham St
Ham
Richmond
Surrey TW10 7HA
Tel 020 8255 6191
Fax 020 8255 6192
E-mail mail@palmcentre.co.uk
Website www.palmcentre.co.uk

Pioneer Nursery
Baldock Lane
Willian
Letchworth
Herts SG6 2AE
Tel 01462 675858
Fax 01462 675596
E-mail pioneer@nursery. dircon.co.uk
Website www.pioneerplants.com
Perennials including a wide range
of tender perennials.

Rickard's Hardy Ferns
Kyre Park
Kyre
Tenbury Wells
Worcestershire WR15 8RP
Tel 01885 410282
Fax 01885 410729

DESIGN AND CONSULTANCY

The Plant Room
47 Barnsbury Street
London N1 1TP
Tel 020 7700 36766
Fax 020 7700 1083
Website www.plantroom.co.uk
Full garden design service. Suppliers
of selected plants and accessories.

LANDSCAPE MATERIALS

Civil Engineering Developments
(CED)
728 London Rd
West Thurrock
Grays
Essex RM20 3NL
Tel 01708 867237
Fax 01708 867230
Suppliers of natural stone paving,
setts, boulders and aggregates.

The Delabole Slate Co.
Pengelly
Delabole
Cornwall PL33 9AZ
Tel 01840 212242
Fax 01840 212948
E-mail info@delaboleslate.com
Website www.delaboleslate.com
Suppliers of blue-grey slate tiles,
paving and boulders.

Granit Union UK Ltd
PO Box 5550
Inverness IVI IWD
Scotland
Tel 07071 472648
Fax 07071 329485
E-mail info@granitunion.com
Website www.granitunion.com
Suppliers of granite setts and
kerbstones in a variety of colours
and finishes.

Silverland Stone
Holloway Hill
Chertsey
Surrey KT16 0AE
Tel 01932 569277
Fax 01932 563558
Suppliers of natural stone
paving, setts, boulders and
aggregates.

Town and Country Paving
Unit 10
Shrublands Nurseries
Roundstone Lane
Angmering
Littlehampton
West Sussex BN16 4AT
Tel 01903 776297
Fax 01903 787637
Specialise in reproduction stone
and terracotta paving.

WATER GARDENING

Butyl Products Ltd
11 Radford Crescent
Billericay
Essex CM12 0DW
Tel 01277 653281
Fax 01277 657921
E-mail
enquiries@butylproducts.co.uk
Flexible pond liners.

Stapeley Water Gardens
London Road
Stapeley
Nantwich
Cheshire CW5 7LH
Tel 01270 623868
Fax 01270 624919
E-mail stapeleywg@btinternet.com
Aquatic plants, pond liners, pumps,
fish etc.

LIGHTING

Garden and Security Lighting
(Division of Light Projects Ltd)
39 Reigate Rd
Hookwood
Horley
Surrey RH6 0HL
Tel 01293 820821
Fax 01293 824052

Outdoor Lighting Supplies
Surrey Business Park
Weston Rd
Epsom
Surrey KT17 1JG
Tel 01372 848818
Fax 01372 848801

IRRIGATION SYSTEMS

**AWS (Automated Watering
Systems Ltd)**
The White House
27 Boundstone Rd
Farnham
Surrey GU10 4TW
Tel 01252 792297
Fax 01252 792297
E-mail
mikey@awsint.freeserve.co.uk

H2O Ltd
Formula House

West Haddon
Northamptonshire NN6 7AU
Tel 01788 510529
Fax 01788 510728

CONSERVATORIES

Amdega
Faverdale
Darlington
Co. Durham DL3 0PW
Tel 01325 468522
Fax 01325 489209
Conservatories and summerhouses.

Trombé
258 Belsize Rd
London NW6 4BT
Tel 020 7316 1849
Fax 020 7316 1838
Website www.trombe.co.uk
Contemporary conservatories.

GARDEN WEBSITES

www.crocus.co.uk
Editorial, plants and accessories.

www.egarden.co.uk
Editorial, plants and accessories.

www.gardenersworld.beeb.com
Editorial, plants, gardening hints
and tips, accessories and events.

www.gardentrouble.com
Problem solving over the internet.

www.greenfingers.com
Editorial, plants and accessories.

www.rhs.org.uk
Fast-expanding site with plant-
finder, details of events and
gardens to visit.

index

acknowledgements

With thanks to:

Barbara Levy, Viv Bowler, Becky Swift, Vicki Vrint, Anna Pavord, Colette Foster, Marisa Merry, Louise Hampden
and all at Catalyst TV, George Plumptre at Greenfingers.com, Mark Latter, Pene Parker, Lisa Pettibone

Sam Joyce and Joanne Carey at The Plant Room

Clive Nichols, Marianne Majerus, Jerry Harpur

Mark Williams, Mark Beretta, Joe Gardner, Dave Hill (garden and security lighting)

Nick McMahon, Alex Gardiner, Adam Caplin, Margaret and Michael Holroyd, Clive Swift, Adam Swift,
Colin and Brenda James, Pat and Sandy Wallace, Paul Thompson, Thursday night footy boys at the Pitz
and Arsene Wenger's red and white army.

**BBC Worldwide would like to thank the following for providing photographs and for permission to reproduce
copyright material. While every effort has been made to trace and acknowledge all copyright holders, we
would like to apologize should there have been any errors or omissions.**

Arcaid pages 76, 84–5 photographer Richard Bryant, 94 Nicholas Kane; **Arcaid/Belle** page 2 photographer Earl Carter, 13 Simon Kenny, 15, 19L Willem Rethmeier; **Nicola Browne** pages 32, 36 designed by Avant Gardener, 41 Ulf Nordfjell, 65 Ian Kirby, 79 Steve Martino, 80–1 Avant Gardener, 102 Ulf Nordfjell, 117R Steve Martino; **The Garden Picture Library** page 12 photographer Steven Wooster, 26R Ron Sutherland, 82 Steven Wooster, 109 and 130 Ron Sutherland; **Harpur Garden Library** page 14 designed by Edwina Von Gal, 23 R. David Adams, 47L Donald Walsh, 47R Grover Dear, 48–9 Barzi and Carares, 50 Oliver Allen, 53L Katie Kend, 53R Val Gerry, 54–5 Galen Lee, 56 Pratial Guttierrez, 58 Keith Corlett, 88 Topher Delaney – San Francisco, CA, 91R Jeff Mendoza, 101, 106 Peter Causer and Roja Dove, 107 Robert Chittock, 110–1 Luciano Giubbelei, 123 R. David Adams, 126–7 Topher Delaney, 133 Jason Payne, 139L Keith Corlett, 140–1 Grover Dear; **The Interior Archive** page 104 photographer Ianthe Ruthven; **Andrew Lawson** page 8 designed by Gordon Taylor and Guy Cooper, 11 Tom Sitta, 59 Gordon Taylor and Guy Cooper, 71 Kate Collity, 112 Christopher Bradley-Hole, 120–1 Ted Smyth, 125 Mark Anthony Walker, 129 Ted Smyth; **Marianne Majerus** pages 16, 19 designed by Joe Swift, 22 Diana Yakeley, 29 Joe Swift, 35 MM, 37 Bunny Guinness (containers Stephen Woodhams), 38 Paul Thompson, 64 Ruth Collier, 67 Thomasina Tarling, 68 Ruth Collier, 72–3 Ward and Benard, 83 Michele Osborne, 98 Christopher Masson, 124 Jill Billington; **New Eden/IPC Syndication** page 9 photographer Sue Wilson, 30, 77, 87, 103, 118 June Buck; **Clive Nichols** page 1 CN, 6 designed by Christopher Bradley-Hole, 21 Joe Swift, 24 Joe Swift and Thamasin Marsh for The Plant Room, 25, 33 Joe Swift, 42 Trevyn McDowell, 45 Robin Cameron Don, 62, 69 Wynniatt-Husey and Clarke, 74 Christopher Bradley-Hole, 89, 92 Wynniatt-Husey and Clarke, 115 Joe Swift, 117L Trevyn McDowell, 135, 137, 139R, 143 Joe Swift, 146–7 Trevyn McDowell, 135, 137, 139R, 143 Joe Swift, 146–7 Trevyn McDowell, 148 Stephen Woodhams, 151, 154, 156, 157 CN, 159 thanks to Architectural Plants, Sussex; **Elizabeth Whiting & Associates** pages 26L photographer Karl-Dietrich Buhler, 44, 96 EWA, 144 Neil Lorimer; **Francesca Yorke** page 61 designed by Nick McMahon and Bunny Bridges

BBC Worldwide would like to thank the Royal Horticultural Society for permission to reproduce the dangerous plant list on pages 160–1. The list is taken from the Conservation and Environment Leaflet, Potentially Harmful Garden Plants, produced by the Royal Horticultural Society. This leaflet is part of a series of useful information leaflets which are produced by the Science and Advice Department at RHS Garden Wisley. The advisory service at RHS Garden Wisley is free to RHS members and is one of the most popular benefits of RHS membership.